Krishnamurti:
REFLECTIONS ON THE SELF

Krishnamurti:
REFLECTIONS ON THE SELF

J. KRISHNAMURTI

Edited by
Raymond Martin

OPEN COURT
Chicago and LaSalle, Illinois

**To order books from Open Court,
call toll free 1-800-815-2280.**

Open Court Publishing Company is a division of Carus Publishing Company.

Copyright © 1997 by Krishnamurti Foundation of America and Krishnamurti Foundation Trust, Ltd.

First printing 1997
Second printing 1998
Third printing 1999

Printed and bound in the United States of America.

Library of Congress Cataloging-in-Publication Data
Krishnamurti, J. (Jiddu), 1895–
    Krishnamurti : reflections on the self/J. Krishnamurti
        p.   cm.
    Includes bibliographical references and index.
    ISBN 0-8126-9355-8 (alk. paper)
    1. Self (Philosophy)   I. Title.
B5134.K753K74   1997   97-3618
126.—dc21   CIP

For additional information about Krishnamurti or his writings, write to:

Krishnamurti Foundation of America
P.O. Box 1560
Ojai, CA 93024, U.S.A.

or

Krishnamurti Foundation Trust, Ltd.
Brockwood Park, Bramdean, Hampshire
SO24 0LQ, U.K.

It is truth that frees, not your
effort to be free.

— Krishnamurti
Ojai, California, 1946

C O N T E N T S

EDITOR'S
PREFACE

*I*N THE SPRING OF 1993 the Krishnamurti Foundation of America asked me to edit a volume of J. Krishnamurti's talks and writings. Their idea was that there should be an anthology that would be particularly interesting to academic philosophers and students of philosophy. The request reminded me of how difficult it had been twenty years earlier for me to understand what Krishnamurti was saying and its relevance to my work as a philosopher. Although I had some misgivings I agreed.

My misgivings were due, first, to the fact that as things stand, Krishnamurti's thought is quite removed from academic philosophy, particularly in the analytic tradition. There is a simple reason why this should be so: Krishnamurti wasn't interested in presenting theories; and theories are what academic philosophy is all about. Second, it seemed—and still seems—to me that my having been an analytic philosopher had actually made it more difficult for me to understand Krishnamurti. The reasons for this are complex and not entirely clear to me even now. I think the heart of the difficulty was that I couldn't understand what Krishnamurti was saying unless what he was saying was 'clear' and it wasn't going to be 'clear' until I had processed it in the way I had been trained as an analytic philosopher to process any view I was considering. As it happens it is hard to process what Krishnamurti is saying in that way. (The problem I was having is analogous, I think, to the problem the Buddhist scholars were having in the "As a Human Being" section below.)

In the end what enabled me to overcome my misgivings about editing this volume was the realization that I'd been moved and instructed by Krishnamurti's thoughts, and in ways that connect directly with my academic interests in philosophy, particularly in the topics of self and personal identity. For instance, Krishnamurti's observations on identification and on the observer/observed distinction are, I think, importantly relevant to post-Parfitian concerns about what matters in survival. And, in my opinion, quite apart from its relevance to academic philosophy, what Krishnamurti has to say is important.

Others had different misgivings. The Krishnamurti Foundation Trust Ltd. (England), in particular, was worried that by my focusing so much on what Krishnamurti had to say about the self and topics directly connected to the self, I might mislead readers into thinking this was all he talked about. It's not all he talked about. The scope of his concerns was extremely broad—as diverse as life itself. The purpose of the present anthology is not to present a balanced view of what Krishnamurti had to say, but only to present that part of it that may be of most immediate interest to philosophers and students of philosophy. Readers may, if they like, seek out other more representative anthologies of Krishnamurti's writings, many of which are available.

The selections that follow not only emphasize certain of Krishnamurti's concerns more than others, they are also heavily edited. The reason for their being so heavily edited is primarily that almost all of what follows is taken from spoken dialogues Krishnamurti had with live audiences. In these dialogues the flow of his thoughts is often interrupted by questions or other audience reactions. In responding, Krishnamurti sometimes goes off in directions perhaps less interesting to the intended audience for this book than his development of his original theme. So, to make the following read well I have edited out most of what, in my opinion, interrupts the orderly flow of Krishnamurti's ideas. Of course, in doing that I may unintentionally have distorted what Krishnamurti was trying to say. My misgivings on this score are eased by the fact that anyone who would like to see what has been edited out can do so easily. The Krishnamurti Foundation Trust has produced a CD-ROM on which is included the complete published works of Krishnamurti, from 1933 to 1986. All of the selections in the current volume are from this source.

Many people have been extremely helpful. Tom Heggestad, in particular, of the Krishnamurti Foundation of America provided both a great deal of technical assistance and also assisted with the selection and editing of texts. Frode Steen, Michael Lommel, Kathleen Quinn, Hilary Rodriguez, Ray McCoy, Rama Rao Pappu, and Mark Lee also made valuable contributions. The idea that there should be such an anthology is due originally to Albion Patterson. Finally, thanks are due to several friends of mine, many of them philosophers or psychologists who had no prior acquaintance with Krishnamurti's writings, who were kind enough to read an early version of the anthology and offer criticisms, suggestions, and encouragement. These include Allen Stairs, Richard Garner, Anna Taam, Michelle Higginbotham, Lynn Bernstein, John Barresi, Tara Brach, Magali Theodore, Stiv Fleishman, Tina Angle, Supriya Goyal, and Udaya.

INTRODUCTION

*I*S IT POSSIBLE TO LIVE without relying psychologically on authority—either on external authority or even on the authority of one's own past experience? For Jiddu Krishnamurti that, suitably qualified, is the key question. His answer is that it is possible and that only in this way can one connect fully with what is real.

Krishnamurti was not a philosopher in the classical sense. He wasn't interested in presenting theories or in arguing for his views. Still what he was up to is continuous with philosophy. Like Socrates, who through his example and questioning encourages his audiences to examine critically the assumptions on which their beliefs depend, Krishnamurti, through his example and questioning, encourages his audiences to examine critically the assumptions on which their very experience of themselves and the world depends. In other words, whereas Socrates encourages what today we would call *critical thinking* (or, simply, *philosophy*), Krishnamurti encourages what we might call *critical looking* (and what he sometimes called *choiceless awareness*).

What Socrates asked the Athenians to do is by now commonplace, at least to philosophers and to students of philosophy. We have learned the lesson he was trying to teach. But to his original audience—the Athenians—what he was asking them to do often must have seemed strange and even pointless. What good could possibly come, many of them must have wondered, from giving the axe to conventional wisdom? Why, they must have asked, should we start freshly when we have accumulated so much? But the distorting weight of what you have accumulated, Socrates tried to point out, is precisely the problem.

At the time Socrates proposed critical thinking there was not much reason for the Athenians to suppose it would bear fruit. But it did. Science is part of that fruit. So is the modern disposition to question the authority of received views.

Have we learned all we need to know about questioning authority? Have we gone far enough? Or is our questioning still seriously limited? Contemporary philosophers and students of philosophy tend to think that we have carried the questioning process about as far as it can go. Many even think we have taken it too far. But up to this point we have questioned mainly only explicit beliefs. In addition to these beliefs might we not still take a great deal that is questionable for granted? And if we do, couldn't this also be an obstacle we need to overcome?

Krishnamurti thought that in our doubting we have not gone far enough. He thought that our questioning is seriously limited and that this is a major obstacle we need to overcome. Could he be right?

Krishnamurti was not the first to propose critical looking. Others, such as the Buddha, had already proposed it. But Krishnamurti's approach was different and perhaps better suited to skeptically minded philosophers and students of philosophy. For one thing, Krishnamurti was anti-authority to a degree that few thinkers have ever been. He had no use for creeds or theories. He discouraged people from examining themselves in an institutional setting or as part of a spiritual discipline. He taught that in examining oneself one should not rely even on what one has learned in previous examinations. The freedom we need to see what is true, he said, is freedom from the known. And because he spoke to us in a contemporary idiom, it may be easier for us to understand what he said.

Krishnamurti had little use for academic philosophy. Occasionally he dismissed it as a waste of time, or worse as a generator of theories that become obstacles in an individual's attempt to understand him or herself. Yet, as the writings in this volume will reveal to those who accept his invitation to examine their experience and behavior, much of what

Krishnamurti said is deeply relevant to philosophy. Its relevance is not that he had theories to propose or critiques of
extant theories. Krishnamurti's focus is on insights. His talent
as a teacher is that he facilitates them. As it happens, many of
the insights he helps his readers to have are centrally relevant
to contemporary philosophy, particularly to theories about
human subjectivity and values. And if indeed he does facilitate insights about the human condition, how could it be
otherwise?

Rather than a theorist, Krishnamurti was a seer and a
teacher. Among the things he thought he saw are certain
inherently distorting psychological structures that bring about
a division in almost everyone's consciousness between "the
observer" and "the observed." This division, he believed, is a
potent source of conflict—both internally for the individual,
and through the individual externalized for society as a whole.
Krishnamurti also proposed a way to remove these damaging
structures, or, more accurately, to facilitate their removal. That
is what the writings in this volume are about: a radical transformation in human consciousness.

Krishnamurti talked a great deal more than he wrote. His
talks—from which almost all of the following selections are
taken—were not lectures but, rather, attempts to engage his
audience in a dialogue in which he and they are wholly
focused on the same aspect of experience or behavior. His
talks were, in effect, guided meditations. That is, they were
attempts by Krishnamurti to go through an experiential
process with his audiences—with you—the result of which is
that something about your understanding of your own experience and its effect on your behavior is clarified. As such, his
talks—here transcribed and edited as if they were writings—
make unusual demands on the reader, especially if the reader
is a philosopher who is accustomed to looking for a theoretical punchline when reading something that seems to put
forth philosophical views. In Krishnamurti's thought, rather
than theoretical punchlines there is an opening to important
insights, for instance, about the nature of identification and

its role in the formation of the self. To have such insights, Krishnamurti suggests, one has to look freshly.

Krishnamurti spoke with a distinctive voice. As an uncompromising enemy of authority, even of the authority of one's own past experience, his focus was on examining current experience directly. Refusing to discuss books or theories, he encouraged people to look at themselves, particularly in their relationships to other people, things, and activities, and he told them just enough about what he thought they would see if they did look to get them going. It is as if through the habit of understanding ourselves in familiar ways we are even at the level of experience stuck in theories. Krishnamurti was—is—extremely good at helping people to get unstuck, that is, at helping them to have insights that break the molds of deeply ingrained patterns of thinking. In other words, his concern was not that his remarks be relevant to theory—although often they are—but that they be relevant to life. His intention was to engage with people who are passionately interested in understanding themselves and the world in which they live. The point of this engagement was to clarify what it means to be oneself and to live in this world. In my opinion, Krishnamurti succeeds in this as few others have.

Philosophers and students of philosophy are surely among those who are passionately interested in understanding themselves and the world. Many of us have devoted much of our lives to this project. We may be surprised, then, to discover how little time and energy we have spent in the sort of inquiry Krishnamurti tried to facilitate. The reason for this is that Krishnamurti's approach to topics of perennial philosophical interest was more meditative than rationally discursive. So, the question for philosophers and students of philosophy in considering how seriously they should take this book, is whether they're willing to try an approach that's philosophical, in a broad sense, but so different from what they're accustomed to doing when they think about or read philosophy that it may be difficult at first for them even to see its relevance. True philosophers are always open to new approaches. Indeed, when an approach has promise, the more radically new it is, the better. This volume is primarily for them.

*   *   *   *   *

By almost any standards, Krishnamurti led a remarkable life. He was born on May 11, 1895, in Madanapalle, India, a small hill-town northwest of Madras, the eighth of eleven children, and one of six to survive into adulthood. His father, a graduate of Madras University, worked for the British Department of Revenue. His mother ran a traditional Brahmin home. At the age of six, Krishnamurti was ritually initiated into Brahminhood and began his formal education. He was not a good student.

When Krishnamurti was ten years old, his mother died. Four years later, in 1909, his father, now retired from the British Administration, secured a job at the headquarters of the Theosophical Society in Adyar, near Madras. In exchange for work, he and four of his sons, including Krishnamurti and his younger brother Nityananda (Nitya), were given accommodation in a cottage outside the beautiful 260-acre Theosophical Society Compound. At the time, all of the children were in poor physical condition.

The Theosophical Society had been founded in New York, thirty-four years earlier, by Madame Blavatsky and Colonel Olcott. Blavatsky claimed to have lived in Tibet and learned occult wisdom from "the Masters." Supposedly the Masters were perfected human beings who periodically appeared on Earth to found a new religion and, through their thoughts and energy, to direct the course of human evolution. In 1882 Blavatsky and Olcott had purchased the estate at Adyar for the society's headquarters. Seven years later, Annie Besant joined the society and a year later she met Charles Leadbeater, a former priest in the Church of England who had joined the society in 1883. Leadbeater was considered to be remarkably psychic. Among other talents, he supposedly saw auras and engaged in astral travel. In 1907, after the deaths of Blavatsky and Olcott and two years prior to Krishnamurti's arrival at the compound, Besant became president of the society.

Central to Theosophy is the teaching that humans are progressively evolving toward universal brotherhood on a path that traverses the sequential appearance of seven root-races. At the origin of each of these races a world-teacher incarnates to impart a spiritual message. The next teacher due to appear was Maitreya, who was thought to be designated for that role by Gautama Buddha. The Theosophist's mission was, in part, to find, raise, and train the child destined to become Maitreya.

In the early summer of 1909, while walking outside the compound, Leadbeater spotted Krishnamurti, who was then fourteen years old. Reportedly overwhelmed by what he took to be Krishnamurti's aura, Leadbeater was sure that Krishnamurti was destined to be a great spiritual teacher. Eventually the Theosophists determined to their own satisfaction that Krishnamurti was to be the physical vehicle for Maitreya. So Krishnamurti and his brother Nitya were brought into the compound, deloused, groomed, and otherwise attended to physically—Krishnamurti's teeth were even straightened. He and Nitya were privately tutored. Eventually Mrs. Besant became Krishnamurti's legal guardian. In 1911 an organization was formed that became the Order of the Star in the East. Its purpose was to herald the arrival of the new world-teacher: Krishnamurti.

For the next ten years Krishnamurti and Nitya were educated in Europe. While in England Krishnamurti became close to Lady Emily Lutyens, whom he regarded as his foster mother, and through whom he was introduced to the life of English aristocracy. He exercised at Sandow's gymnasium, attended ballet, film, theater, visited art galleries, and traveled extensively. During this period he became a scratch golfer and learned how to assemble and reassemble an automobile engine. He also read widely, among other authors, Stephen Leacock, P. G. Wodehouse, Turgenev, Dostoevsky, Nietzsche,

Bergson, Shelley, and Keats. In 1921 Krishnamurti went to Paris where he took courses at the Sorbonne and studied Sanskrit.

In 1922, Krishnamurti and Nitya moved to Ojai, California, where, it was hoped, the dry climate would help Nitya in his battle with tuberculosis. During the summer of that year, shortly after he began to meditate daily, Krishnamurti had a life-transforming experience, which he described, in part, as follows:

> There was a man mending the road; that man was myself; the pickaxe he held was myself; the very stone which he was break-ing up was a part of me; the tender blade of grass was my very being, and the tree beside the man was myself.[1]

The next day, while sitting under a nearby pepper tree, he had additional experiences, after which he wrote:

> I was supremely happy, for I had seen. Nothing could ever be the same. . . . I had touched compassion which heals all sorrow and suffering; it is not for myself, but for the world. I have stood on the mountain top and gazed at the mighty Beings. Never can I be in utter darkness; I have seen the glorious and healing Light. The fountain of truth has been revealed to me and the darkness has been dispersed. Love in all its glory has intoxicated my heart; my heart can never be closed. I have drunk at the fountain of Joy and eternal Beauty.[2]

Krishnamurti described himself as "God-intoxicated."

In November of 1925 Nitya died and Krishnamurti expe-rienced what seems to have been the profoundest grief of his life.

During the next few years Krishnamurti distanced himself from Theosophy and also developed some of the distinctive motifs of his own subsequent teachings. The decisive break with Theosophy came in August of 1929, when in the pres-ence of three thousand members of the society he dissolved the Order of the Star and in the process staked out his own mission:

I maintain that truth is a pathless land, and you cannot approach it by any path whatsoever, by any religion, by any sect. That is my point of view, and I adhere to that absolutely and unconditionally. Truth, being limitless, unconditioned, unapproachable by any path whatsoever, cannot be organized; nor should any organization be formed to lead or coerce people along any particular path. . . . You will probably form other Orders, you will continue to belong to other organizations searching for truth. . . . If an organization be created for this purpose, it becomes a crutch, a weakness, a bondage, and must cripple the individual, and prevent him from growing, from establishing his uniqueness, which lies in the discovery for himself of that absolute, unconditioned truth. . . . Because I am free, unconditioned, whole, not the part, not the relative, but the whole truth that is eternal, I desire those, who seek to understand me, to be free, not to follow me, not to make out of me a cage which will become a religion, a sect. . . . I have now decided to disband the Order, as I happen to be its Head. You can form other organizations and expect someone else. With that I am not concerned, nor with creating new cages, new decorations for those cages. My only concern is to set men absolutely, unconditionally free.[3]

The next year, in 1930, Krishnamurti formally resigned from the Theosophical Society.

In 1931, Krishnamurti returned to Ojai to rest, meditate, and think. During this time he wrote to Lady Emily of the difficulty of putting what he wanted to say into words. However, once he did start again to write and speak he was remarkably consistent.

From 1933 to 1939 Krishnamurti traveled extensively, talking to large audiences. During the war he was unable to travel and led a life of relative seclusion at Ojai, although he still met with many visitors. He became close friends with Aldous Huxley, who encouraged him to write. After the war, Krishnamurti resumed his traveling and talking. During the last forty years of his life, he gave, on average, about one hundred talks a year, often to audiences of several thousand people. He also engaged in personal and small-group discussions with those who came to see him. On one light-hearted occasion during this period, he went on a picnic in California, with Bertrand Russell, Charlie Chaplin, Greta Garbo, Aldous Huxley, and Christopher Isherwood; a local sheriff evicted them from their chosen picnic site, not believing them to be who they said they were.

In 1953, Krishnamurti wrote *Education and the Significance of Life*, followed in 1954 by *The First and Last Freedom*, which included a foreword by Huxley. Then there appeared three volumes entitled *Commentaries on Living*. He also wrote *Krishnamurti's Notebook*, a personal journal mostly from 1961; *Krishnamurti's Journal*, from writings he had done in 1973 and 1975; two volumes of letters to the schools started in his name; and *Krishnamurti to Himself*, his last (audiotaped) journal, in 1983.

The remainder of Krishnamurti's books (the number is now over one hundred and still growing) are edited transcriptions of talks and discussions held by him in various parts of the world. The discussants are mostly everyday people but often also include well-known people, such as the Nobel laureates Maurice Wilkins and Jonas Salk, theoretical physicist David Bohm, and the Buddhist scholar Walpola Rahula. Videotapes of many of these discussions are available. Excerpts from these videotapes are included in several films that have been made about Krishnamurti, including *Krishnamurti: The Challenge of Change* and *The Seer Who Walks Alone*. In addition Krishnamurti's talks and public discussions, from 1933 to 1986, are available on CD-ROM.

On February 17, 1986, in Ojai, California, at the age of ninety, Krishnamurti died of pancreatic cancer.

RAYMOND MARTIN
UNIVERSITY OF MARYLAND

Inquiry

DIALOGUE

A LECTURE GENERALLY MEANS telling or explaining a certain subject, for you to be instructed, to learn. This is not a lecture. Here, we are having a conversation together like two friends, perhaps walking in a quiet lane, full of trees and beauty of flowers, the singing of many birds, sitting down on a bench unfrequented, solitary and having a dialogue, because we are concerned, both you and the speaker, with our daily life, not with something beyond, romantic and fantastic. Because if we don't make our own lives clear, unruffled, nonchaotic, whatever we may do, it will have no meaning.

So we must begin very near to go far. The near is what we are. Please, if one may point out, it is your responsibility to think together, not to accept; because one must have a great deal of skepticism, a skepticism that is not trammeled by fear, a doubt so that one begins to question not only what the speaker is saying but also what you think, what you believe, your faith, your conclusions, your religion. One must have tremendous questioning, doubt, inquiry, through deep exploration, not accepting, because throughout the world, religion has played an extraordinary part in narrowing the mind, in narrowing investigation. We are together going to look at many things that confront our daily life. We are not going to talk about any philosophy, any dogma, or encourage any faith, but with a mind that is questioning, doubting, demanding, find out for ourselves what is true, what is illusory, what is fantastic, and what is false.[4]

*T*HERE ARE CERTAIN THINGS which must be taken for granted. First we must understand what we mean by communication, what the word means to each one of us, what is

2

involved in it, what is its structure, its nature. If two of us, you and I, are to communicate with each other there must be not only a verbal understanding of what is being said, at the intellectual level, but also, by implication, listening and learning. These two things are essential in order that we may communicate with each other: listening and learning.

Secondly, each one of us has, obviously, a background of knowledge, prejudice, and experience, also the suffering and the innumerable complex issues involved in relationship. That is the background of most of us and with that background we try to listen. After all, each one of us is the result of our culturally complex life—we are the result of the whole culture of man, with the education and the experiences, not only of a few years, but of centuries.

I do not know if you have ever examined how you listen, it doesn't matter to what, whether to a bird, to the wind in the leaves, to the rushing waters, or how you listen to a dialogue with yourself, to your conversation in various relationships with your intimate friends, your wife or husband. If we *try* to listen, we find it extraordinarily difficult, because we are always projecting our opinions and ideas, our prejudices, our background, our inclinations, our impulses; when they dominate we hardly listen to what is being said. In that state there is no value at all. One listens and therefore learns, only in a state of attention, a state of silence in which this whole background is in abeyance, is quiet. Then, it seems to me, it is possible to communicate.

Several other things are involved. If you listen with the background or image that you may have created about the speaker, and listen as to one with certain authority—which the speaker may or may not have—then obviously you are not listening. You are listening to the projection which you have put forward and that prevents you from listening. So again, communication is not possible. Obviously, real communication or communion can only take place when there is silence. When two people are intent, seriously, to understand something, bringing their whole mind and heart, their nerves, their eyes, their ears, to understand, then in that attention there is a certain quality of silence; then actual communication, actual communion, takes place. In that there is not only learning but complete understanding—and that understanding is not something different from immediate action. That is to say, when one listens without any intention, without any barrier, putting aside all opinions, conclusions, experiences—then, in that state one not only understands whether what is being said is true or false, but if it is true there is immediate action, and if it is false there is no action at all.[5]

WHAT WE WILL BE DISCUSSING IS THIS: how are we to recognize the various activities of the self and its subtle forms behind which the mind takes shelter? We see the self, its activity and its action based on an idea. Action based on an idea is a form of the self because it gives continuity to that action, a purpose to that action. So, idea in action becomes the means of continuing the self. If the idea was not there, action has a different meaning altogether, which is not born of the self. The search for power, position, authority, ambition, and all the rest are the forms of the self in all its different ways. But what is important is to understand the self and I am sure you and I are convinced of it. If I may add here, let us be earnest about this matter; because I feel that if you and I as individuals, not as a group of people belonging to certain classes, certain societies, certain climatic divisions, can understand this and act upon this, then I think there will be real revolution. The moment it becomes universal and better organized, the self takes shelter in that; whereas, if you and I as individuals can love, can carry this out actually in everyday life, then the revolution that is so essential will come into being, not because you organized it by the coming together of various groups, but because, individually, there is revolution taking place all the time.[6]

AUTHORITY

I FEEL VERY STRONGLY THAT each one of us, being responsible for the chaos, misery, and sorrow in the world, as a human being must bring about a radical revolution in himself. Because each in himself is both the society and the individual, he is both violence and peace, he is this strange mixture of pleasure and hate and fear, aggressiveness, domination, and gentleness. Sometimes one predominates over the other and there is a great deal of unbalance in all of us.

We are responsible not only to the world but also for ourselves, what we do, what we think, how we act, how we feel. Merely to seek truth or pleasure without understanding this strange mixture, this strange contradiction of violence and gentleness, of affection and brutality, of jealousy, of greed, envy, and anxiety, has very little meaning. Unless there is a radical transformation in the very foundation of ourselves, merely to seek great pleasure or to seek truth has very little meaning. Man has sought that thing we call truth, apparently, throughout historical times and before, an otherness which we call God, which we call the timeless state, a thing which is not measurable, which is not nameable. Man has always sought that because his life is very dull. There is always death, old age, there is so much pain, contradiction, conflict, a sense of utter boredom, a meaninglessness to life. We are caught in that and to escape from it—or because we have slightly understood this complex existence—we want to find something more, something that won't be destroyed by time, by thought, by any human corruption. And man has always sought that and, not finding it, he has cultivated faith—faith in a god, in a savior, faith in an idea.

I do not know if you have noticed that faith invariably breeds violence. Do consider this. When I have faith in an

5

idea, in a concept, I want to protect that idea, I want to protect that concept, that symbol; that symbol, that idea, that ideology is a projection of myself, I am identified with it and I want to protect it at any price. And when I defend something I must be violent. And more and more, as one observes, faith has no place anymore; nobody believes in anything anymore—thank God. Either one becomes cynical and bitter, or one invents a philosophy which will be satisfactory intellectually—but the central problem is not resolved.

The central problem is really: how is one to bring about a fundamental mutation in this complex, unhappy world of confusion, not only outside but inside—a world of contradiction, a world of such anxiety. Then, when there is a mutation, one can go further, if one wants. But without that radical, fundamental change every effort to go beyond that has no meaning. The search for truth and the question as to whether there is a god or not, whether there is a timeless dimension, will be answered—not by another, not by a priest, not by a savior—by nobody but yourself and you will be able to answer that question for yourself only when there is this mutation that can and must take place in every human being. That is what we are interested in and concerned with in all these talks. We are concerned not only as to how to bring about a change objectively in this miserable world outside of us, but also in ourselves. Most of us are so unbalanced, most of us are so violent, greedy, and are hurt so easily when anything goes against us, that it seems to me the fundamental issue is: what can a human being—such as you and I—living in this world, do?

If you seriously put that question to yourself I wonder what you would answer—is there anything to be done at all? You know, we are asking a very serious question. As human beings, you and I, what can we do, not only to change the world but ourselves—what can we do? Will somebody tell us? People have told us; the priests who are supposed to understand these things better than laymen like us, they have told us and that hasn't led us very far. We have the most sophisticated human beings, even they have not led us very far.

We cannot depend on anybody, there is no guide, there is no teacher, there is no authority, there is only oneself and one's relationship with another and the world, there is nothing else. When one realizes that, faces that, either it brings great despair from which comes cynicism, bitterness, and all the rest of it, or in facing it, one realizes that one is totally responsible for oneself and for the world, nobody else; when one faces that all self-pity goes. Most of us thrive on self-pity, blaming others, and this occupation doesn't bring clarity.

What you and I can do, to live in this world sanely, healthily, logically, rationally, but also inwardly to have great balance, to live without any conflict, without any hate, without any violence, seems to me to be a question which each of us has to answer for himself.[7]

MOST OF US LISTEN TO BE TOLD WHAT TO DO, or to conform to a new pattern, or we listen merely to gather further information. If we are here with any such attitude, then the process of listening will have very little significance in what we are trying to do in these talks. And I am afraid most of us are only concerned with that: we want to be told, we are listening in order to be taught; and a mind that merely wants to be told is obviously incapable of learning.

I think there is a process of learning which is not related to wanting to be taught. Being confused, most of us want to find someone who will help us not to be confused, and therefore we are merely learning or acquiring knowledge in order to conform to a particular pattern; and it seems to me that all such forms of learning must invariably lead not only to further confusion, but also to deterioration of the mind. I think there is a different kind of learning, a learning which is an inquiry into ourselves and in which there is no teacher and no taught, neither the disciple nor the guru. When you begin to inquire into the operation of your own mind, when you observe your own thinking, your daily activities and feelings, you cannot be taught because there is no one to teach you. You cannot base your inquiry on any authority, on any assumption, on any previous knowledge. If you do, then you are merely conforming to the pattern of what you already know, and therefore you are no longer learning about yourself.[8]

ONE ACCEPTS VERY EASILY the path that is the most satisfying, the most convenient, the most pleasurable. It is very easy to move into that groove. And authority dictates, lays down, in a religious or a psychological system, a method by which, or through which, you are told you will find security. But if one sees that there is no security in any such authority, then one can find out whether it is possible to live without any guidance, without any control, without any effort psychologically. So, one is going to investigate, to see, whether the mind can be free to find the truth of this matter, so that one will never, under any circumstance, conform to any pattern of authority, psychologically.

This is asking a tremendous lot. Because we are educated, conditioned to accept authority because that is the most convenient and the easiest way to live. Put all our faith and all our trust in somebody, or in some idea, or in some conclusion, or in some teaching, and give ourselves to that, hoping that we shall find some deep satisfaction, deep security—the guru, those teachings have done all the work and you just have to follow!

Now an intelligent person, fairly aware, awakened in the normal sense, objects to that totally. Living in a free country like this where there is freedom of speech and so on, you would object tremendously to a totalitarian state; but you would accept the authority of psychologists, the guru, the teachings that would promise you something marvelous in the future, but not now; you'd accept all that because it is very satisfactory. So we are going to demolish all that—if you are willing—because otherwise you will not be able to awaken that intelligence of which we are talking.

Where there is authority, psychologically, there is conformity: to conform to the pattern set by another through various sanctions, or the authority of your own which you have experienced, which you have felt and from that conclude and have security in that conclusion. Is there any security in psychological authority, in any teachings—including the speaker's teachings, the so-called religious teachings and the top guru's, you know, all that stuff!—is there any security in all that? And yet if you observe, millions and millions are following that path, that way of thinking, hoping that eventually some day, in some future life, or somewhere there is going to be security. Now we are going to question and ask ourselves if in it there is any kind of truth.

Please, we are working together—right? We are exploring together. We are really thinking out this problem together, so that I am not thinking and you merely listening, but we are sharing the thing together to find out the truth of this enormous weight that man has carried hoping thereby to find somewhere some security and happiness. Please, it is your responsibility as well as the speaker's to go into this question very, very carefully, to find out whether one can live a daily life, a nonconforming life, non-imitative life, not following any particular tradition, because if you have got a tradition, a sanction, a pattern, you will invariably conform to that, consciously, or unconsciously.

When one is conforming to a pattern, religious, psychological, or the pattern which one has set for oneself, there is always a contradiction between what one actually is and the pattern. There is always a conflict and this conflict is endless. If one has finished with one pattern one goes to another. One is educated to live in this field of conflict because of these ideals, patterns, conclusions, beliefs, and so on. Conforming to a pattern one is never free; one does not know what compassion is and one is always battling and therefore giving importance to oneself; the self becomes extraordinarily important with the idea of self-improvement.

So, is it possible to live without a pattern?—the pattern being tradition, a conclusion, an ideal, an assumption that there is a divinity which will help you in the future to evolve and so on—you know, all that business. Now, how is one, as a human being, the total representative of all mankind, how is one going to find out the truth of this matter? Because if one's consciousness is changed radically, profoundly—no, revolutionized rather than changed—then one affects the consciousness of the whole of mankind. Please see the truth of this, then you become tremendously responsible, then you are not just worrying a little bit about your own particular little worry, whether you have a little sex, or no sex, or should smoke, or not smoke—you know all those kinds of petty little affairs.

We are going to see, investigate together, whether there is a life in which there is not a spark of authority. How is one going to go into this problem; with what capacity does one investigate? To investigate there must be freedom from motive. If one wants to investigate the question of authority, one's background says: I must obey, I must follow; and in the process one's background is always projecting, is always distorting one's investigation. Can one be free of one's background so that it does not interfere in any way with one's investigation?

One's urgency to find the truth, one's immediacy, one's demand, puts the background in abeyance; one's intensity to find out is so strong that the background ceases to interfere. Although the background, one's education, one's conditioning, is so strong—it has accumulated for centuries; consciously one cannot fight it, one cannot push it aside; one cannot battle with it and one sees that to fight the background only intensifies the background—yet one's very intensity to find out the truth of authority puts that background much further away; it is no longer impinging on one's mind.

Are you prepared to investigate this whole question of psychological, external, imposed authority of human beings by other human beings, to find the truth of it? Which means to find the truth there must be no motive, no cause for the investigation into the truth of authority. This is asking a tremendous lot, isn't it? Are we prepared for this? Or are we all too old? It doesn't matter. If you are too old it is your affair, if you are not intense it is your affair.

I want to find out the truth of it, as a human being. Assuming I am a representative of human beings, I say to myself I want to find the truth of this matter, which is: whether one can live a life without any conformity, without any conflict, without having a goal, a purpose, a projected ideal, which all creates, brings about, conflict. The intensity of the investigation depends on the urgency to find the truth of it, to have tremendous energy to find out.[9]

ON PAPER WE CAN DRAW a blueprint for a brilliant utopia, a brave new world; but the sacrifice of the present to an unknown future will certainly never solve any of our problems. There are so many elements intervening between now and the future, that no one can know what the future will be. What we can and must do if we are in earnest, is to tackle our problems now, and not postpone them to the future. Eternity is not in the future; eternity is now. Our problems exist in the present, and it is only in the present that they can be solved.

Those of us who are serious must regenerate ourselves; but there can be regeneration only when we break away from those values which we have created through our self-protective and aggressive desires. Self-knowledge is the beginning of freedom, and it is only when we know ourselves that we can bring about order and peace.

Now, some may ask, "What can a single individual do that will affect history? Can he accomplish anything at all by the way he lives?" Certainly he can. You and I are obviously not going to stop the immediate wars, or create an instantaneous understanding between nations; but at least we can bring about, in the world of our everyday relationships, a fundamental change which will have its own effect.

Individual enlightenment does affect large groups of people, but only if one is not eager for results. If one thinks in terms of gain and effect, right transformation of oneself is not possible.

Human problems are not simple, they are very complex. To understand them requires patience and insight, and it is of the highest importance that we as individuals understand and

11

resolve them for ourselves. They are not to be understood through easy formulas or slogans; nor can they be solved at their own level by specialists working along a particular line, which only leads to further confusion and misery. Our many problems can be understood and resolved only when we are aware of ourselves as a total process, that is, when we understand our whole psychological make-up; and no religious or political leader can give us the key to that understanding.

To understand ourselves, we must be aware of our relationship, not only with people, but also with property, with ideas, and with nature. If we are to bring about a true revolution in human relationship, which is the basis of all society, there must be a fundamental change in our own values and outlook; but we avoid the necessary and fundamental transformation of ourselves and try to bring about political revolutions in the world, which always leads to bloodshed and disaster.

Relationship based on sensation can never be a means of release from the self; yet most of our relationships are based on sensation, they are the outcome of our desire for personal advantage, for comfort, for psychological security. Though they may offer us a momentary escape from the self, such relationships only give strength to the self, with its enclosing and binding activities. Relationship is a mirror in which the self and all its activities can be seen; and it is only when the ways of the self are understood in the reactions of relationship that there is creative release from the self.

Ignorance is lack of knowledge of the ways of the self, and this ignorance cannot be dissipated by superficial activities and reforms; it can be dissipated only by one's constant awareness of the movements and responses of the self in all its relationships.

What we must realize is that we are not only conditioned by environment, but that we are the environment—we are not something apart from it. Our thoughts and responses are conditioned by the values which society, of which we are a part, has imposed upon us.

We never see that we are the total environment because there are several entities in us, all revolving around the 'me', the self. The self is made up of these entities, which are merely desires in various forms. From this conglomeration of desires arises the central figure, the thinker, the will of the 'me' and the 'mine', and a division is thus established between the self and the not-self, between the 'me' and the environment or society. This separation is the beginning of conflict, inward and outward.

Awareness of this whole process, both the conscious and the hidden, is meditation; and through this meditation the self, with its desires and conflicts, is transcended. Self-knowledge is necessary if one is to be free of the influences and values that give shelter to the self; and in this freedom alone is there creation, truth, God, or what you will.

Opinion and tradition mold our thoughts and feelings from the tenderest age. The immediate influences and impressions produce an effect which is powerful and lasting, and which shapes the whole course of our conscious and unconscious life. Conformity begins in childhood through education and the impact of society.

The desire to imitate is a very strong factor in our life, not only at the superficial levels, but also profoundly. We have hardly any independent thoughts and feelings. When they do occur, they are mere reactions and are therefore not free from the established pattern; for there is no freedom in reaction.

Philosophy and religion lay down certain methods whereby we can come to the realization of truth or God; yet merely to follow a method is to remain thoughtless and unin-tegrated, however beneficial the method may seem to be in our daily social life.

The urge to conform, which is the desire for security, breeds fear and brings to the fore the political and religious authorities, the leaders and heroes who encourage sub-servience and by whom we are subtly or grossly dominated; but not to conform is only a reaction against authority and in no way helps us to become integrated human beings. Reaction is endless, it only leads to further reaction.

Conformity, with its undercurrent of fear, is a hindrance; but mere intellectual recognition of this fact will not resolve the hindrance. It is only when we are aware of hindrances with our whole being that we can be free of them without creating further and deeper blockages.

When we are inwardly dependent, then tradition has a great hold on us; and a mind that thinks along traditional lines cannot discover that which is new. By conforming we become mediocre imitators, cogs in a cruel social machine. It is what we think that matters, not what others want us to think. When we conform to tradition, we soon become mere copies of what we should be.

This imitation of what we should be breeds fear, and fear kills creative thinking. Fear dulls the mind and heart so that we are not alert to the whole significance of life; we become insensitive to our own sorrows, to the movement of the birds, to the smiles and miseries of others.

Conscious and unconscious fear has many different causes, and it needs alert watchfulness to be rid of them all. Fear cannot be eliminated through discipline, sublimation, or through any other act of will: its causes have to be searched out and understood. This needs patience and an awareness in which there is no judgment of any kind.

It is comparatively easy to understand and dissolve our conscious fears. But unconscious fears are not even discovered by most of us, for we do not allow them to come to the surface; and when on rare occasions they do come to the surface, we hasten to cover them up, to escape from them. Hidden fears often make their presence known through dreams and other forms of intimation, and they cause greater deterioration and conflict than do the superficial fears.

Our lives are not just on the surface, their greater part is concealed from casual observation. If we would have our obscure fears come into the open and dissolve, the conscious mind must be somewhat still, not everlastingly occupied; then, as these fears come to the surface, they must be observed without hindrance, for any form of condemnation or justification only strengthens fear. To be free from all fear, we must be awake to its darkening influence, and only constant watchfulness can reveal its many causes.

One of the results of fear is the acceptance of authority in human affairs. Authority is created by our desire to be right, to be secure, to be comfortable, to have no conscious conflicts or disturbances; but nothing which results from fear can help us to understand our problems, even though fear may take the form of respect and submission to the so-called wise.

The wise wield no authority, and those in authority are not wise. Fear in whatever form prevents the understanding of ourselves and of our relationship to all things.

The following of authority is the denial of intelligence. To accept authority is to submit to domination, to subjugate oneself to an individual, to a group, or to an ideology, whether religious or political; and this subjugation of oneself to authority is the denial, not only of intelligence, but also of individual freedom. Compliance with a creed or a system of ideas is a self-protective reaction. The acceptance of authority may help us temporarily to cover up our difficulties and problems; but to avoid a problem is only to intensify it, and in the process, self-knowledge and freedom are abandoned.

How can there be compromise between freedom and the acceptance of authority? If there is compromise, then those who say they are seeking self-knowledge and freedom are not earnest in their endeavor. We seem to think that freedom is an ultimate end, a goal, and that in order to become free we must first submit ourselves to various forms of suppression and intimidation. We hope to achieve freedom through conformity; but are not the means as important as the end? Do not the means shape the end?

To have peace, one must employ peaceful means; for if the means are violent, how can the end be peaceful? If the end is freedom, the beginning must be free, for the end and the beginning are one. There can be self-knowledge and intelligence only when there is freedom at the very outset; and freedom is denied by the acceptance of authority.

We worship authority in various forms: knowledge, success, power, and so on. We exert authority on the young, and at the same time we are afraid of superior authority. When man himself has no inward vision, outward power and position assume vast importance, and then the individual is more and more subject to authority and compulsion, he becomes the instrument of others. We can see this process going on around us: in moments of crisis, the democratic nations act like the totalitarian, forgetting their democracy and forcing man to conform.

If we can understand the compulsion behind our desire to dominate or to be dominated, then perhaps we can be free from the crippling effects of authority. We crave to be certain, to be right, to be successful, to know; and this desire for certainty, for permanence, builds up within ourselves the authority of personal experience, while outwardly it creates the authority of society, of the family, of religion, and so on. But merely to ignore authority, to shake off its outward symbols, is of very little significance.

To break away from one tradition and conform to another, to leave this leader and follow that, is but a superficial gesture. If we are to be aware of the whole process of authority, if we are to see the inwardness of it, if we are to understand and transcend the desire for certainty, then we must have extensive awareness and insight; we must be free, not at the end, but at the beginning.

The craving for certainty, for security, is one of the major activities of the self, and it is this compelling urge that has to be constantly watched, and not merely twisted or forced in another direction, or made to conform to a desired pattern. The self, the 'me' and the 'mine', is very strong in most of us; sleeping or waking, it is ever alert, always strengthening itself. But when there is an awareness of the self and a realization that all its activities, however subtle, must inevitably lead to conflict and pain, then the craving for certainty, for self-continuance, comes to an end.

One has to be constantly watchful for the self to reveal its ways and tricks; but when we begin to understand them, and to understand the implications of authority and all that is involved in our acceptance and denial of it, then we are already disentangling ourselves from authority.[10]

TO MOST OF US, the problems of life are not very serious, and we want ready-made answers. We do not want to delve into the problem, we do not want to think it out completely, fully, and understand the whole significance of it; we want to be told the answer, and the more gratifying the answer, the quicker we accept it. When we are made to think about a problem, when we have to go into it, our minds rebel, because we are not used to inquiring into problems.

In considering these questions, if you merely wait for a ready-made answer from me, I am afraid you will be disappointed; but if we can go into the question together, think it out anew, not according to old patterns, then perhaps we shall be able to solve the many problems which confront us, and which we are usually so unwilling to look at. We have to look at them, that is, there must be the capacity to face the fact; and we cannot face the fact, whatever it be, as long as we have explanations, as long as words fill our minds.

It is words, explanations, memories, that cloud the understanding of the fact. The fact is always new, because the fact is a challenge; but the fact ceases to be a challenge, it is not new, when we consider it merely as the old and discard it. So, in considering these questions, I hope you and I will think out the problem together. I am not laying down the answer, but we are going to think out each problem together and discover the truth of it.

Questioner: You are preaching a kind of philosophical anarchism, which is the favorite escape of the highbrow intellectuals. Will not a community always need some form of regulation and authority? What social order could express the values you are upholding?

Krishnamurti: Sir, when life is very difficult, when problems are increasing, we escape either through the intellect or through mysticism. We know the escape through the intellect: rationalization, more and more cunning devices, more and more technique, more and more economic responses to life, all very subtle and intellectual. And there is the escape through mysticism, through the sacred books, through worshiping an established idea—idea being an image, a symbol, a superior entity, or what you will—thinking that it is not of the mind; but both the intellectual and the mystic are products of the mind.

One we call the intellectual highbrow, and the other we despise, because it is the fashion now to despise the mystic, to kick him out; but both function through the mind. The intellectual may be able to talk, to express himself more clearly, but he too withdraws himself into his own ideas and lives there quietly, disregarding society and pursuing his illusions, which are born of the mind; so I do not think there is any difference between the two. They are both pursuing illusions of the mind, and neither the highbrow nor the lowbrow, neither the mystic, the yogi who escapes, withdraws from the world, nor the commissar, has the answer.

It is you and I, ordinary common people, who have to solve this problem without being highbrow or mystical, without escaping either through rationalization, or through vague terms and getting hypnotized by words, by methods of our own self-projection.

What you are the world is, and unless you understand yourself, what you create will always increase confusion and misery; but the understanding of yourself is not a process through which you have to go in order to act. It is not that you must first understand yourself and then act; on the contrary the understanding of yourself is in the very action of relationship. Action is relationship in which you understand yourself, in which you see yourself clearly; but if you wait to become perfect or to understand yourself, that waiting is dying. Most of us have been active, and that activity has left us empty, dry; and once we have been bitten, we wait and do not act further, because we say, "I won't act until I understand."

Waiting to understand is a process of death; but if you understand the whole problem of action, of living from moment to moment, which does not demand waiting, then understanding is in what you are doing, it is in action itself, it is not separate from living. Living is action, living is relationship, and because we do not understand relationship, because we avoid relationship, we are caught in words; and words have mesmerized us into action that leads to further chaos and misery.

Q: Will not a community always need some form of regulation and authority?

K: Obviously there must be authority as long as a community is based on violence. Is not our present social structure based on violence, on intolerance? The community is you and another in relationship; and is not your relationship based on violence? Are you not ultimately out for yourself? Is not our present relationship based on violence—violence being the process of self-enclosure, isolation? Is not our daily action a process of isolation? And since each one is isolating himself, there must be authority to bring about cohesion, either the authority of the state, or the authority of organized religion.

To the extent that we have been held together at all, we have been held so far through fear of religion or through fear of government; but a man who understands relationship, whose life is not based on violence, has no need for authority. The man who needs authority is the stupid man, the violent man, the unhappy man—which is yourself.

You seek authority because you think that without it you are lost; that is why you have all these religions, illusions, and beliefs, that is why you have innumerable leaders, political as well as religious. In moments of confusion you produce the leader, and that leader you follow; and since he is the outcome of your own confusion, obviously the leader himself must be confused. So, authority is necessary as long as you are producing conflict, misery, and violence in your relationships.

Q: What social order could express the values you are upholding?

K: Sir, do you understand what values I am upholding? Am I upholding anything—at least, for those few who have listened with serious intention? I am not giving you a new set of values for an old set of values, I am not giving you a substitution; but I say: look at the very things that you hold, examine them, search out their truth, and the values that you then establish will create the new society. It is not for somebody else to draw up a blueprint which you can follow blindly without knowing what it is all about, but it is for you to find out for yourself the value, the truth of each problem.

What I am saying is very clear and simple if you will follow it. Society is your own product, it is your projection. The world's problem is your problem, and to understand that problem you have to understand yourself; and you can understand yourself only in relationship, not in escapes. Because you escape through them, your religion, your knowledge have no validity, no significance. You are unwilling to alter fundamentally your relationship with another because that means trouble, that means disturbance, revolution; so you talk about the highbrow intellectual, the mystic, and all the rest of that nonsense.

A new society, a new order, cannot be established by another; it must be established by you. A revolution based on an idea is not a revolution at all. Real revolution comes from within, and that revolution is not brought about through escape, but comes only when you understand your relationships, your daily activities, the way you are acting, the way you are thinking, the way you are talking, your attitude to your neighbor, to your wife, to your husband, to your children. Without understanding yourself, whatever you do, however far you may escape will only produce more misery, more wars, more destruction.[11]

AS A HUMAN
BEING

I AM HERE, AN ORDINARY HUMAN BEING. I have not read a thing. I want to know. Where am I to begin? I have to work: in a garden, as a cook, in a factory, an office; I have to work. And also there are the wife and children: I love them, I hate them, I am a sexual addict because that is the only escape offered to me in life. Here I am. That is my map of life and I start from here. I cannot start from over there; I start here and I ask myself what it is all about.

I know nothing about God. You can invent, pretend; I have a horror of pretending. If I do not know, I do not know. I am not going to quote Shankara, Buddha, or anybody. So I say: this is where I start. Can I bring about order in my life?—order, not invented by me or by them, but order that is virtue. Can I bring it about? And to be virtuous there must be no battle, no conflict in me or outside. Therefore, there must be no aggressiveness, no violence, no hate, no animosity. And I find out I am afraid. I must be free of fear. To be conscious of it is to be aware of all this, aware of where I am.

And then I find out I can be alone—not carry all the burdens of memory. I can be alone because I have understood order in my life; and I have understood order because I have denied disorder, because I have learned about disorder. Disorder means conflict, acceptance of authority, complying, imitation, all that. That is disorder, the social morality is disorder. Out of that I will bring order in myself; not myself as a petty little human being in a backyard, but as a Human Being.

Every human being is going through this hell. So if I, as a human being, understand this, I have discovered something that all human beings can discover.[12]

*K*rishnamurti: So what is the self? The whole process of identification: my house, my name, my possessions, what I will be, the success, the power, the position, the prestige—the identification process is the essence of the self.

Can this identification come to an end if thought doesn't identify itself with possessions, because identification gives it pleasure, position, security? The root of the self is the movement of thought.

When thought comes to an end, that is a form of death while living. Now, can thought come to an end? Every human being has identified himself and so conditioned himself with something or other. While living can that death, which is the end of thought, take place?

Walpola Rahula: I agree when you say it is not necessary to wait until the end of your life. Buddha pointed out the same thing when this question was put to him. When asked what would happen to the Buddha after his death, he asked the disciple, "What is Buddha? Is it this body?"—just as you asked about the name, the form, exactly what you said. In Buddhist terminology, this is called the *kamarupa*.

K: Sir, if I may ask, I hope you don't think me impudent—why do we bring in the Buddha? We are talking as human beings.

WR: Just because I raised the question from the Buddha's point of view.

K: Ah, no, as a human being I want to know: can one live in daily life without the self?

WR: Of course, my question was not that. The question is what happens to the person who has realized the truth, who has become liberated, free.

K: I would never ask that question, because he might say this happens, or he might say that happens, or nothing happens. Then it becomes a theory to me, which is an idea.

WR: I wanted from you a little more than that.

K: Ah, you want from me.

WR: Not a theory.

K: If you want it from this person who is talking, you have to inquire as he is inquiring. And therefore he asks: is it possible to live in daily life—not at the end of one's existence, in daily life—without this identification process, which brings about the structure and the nature of the self, which is the result of thought?

Can the movement of thought end while I am living? That is the question, rather than what happens when I die. The 'me' is merely a movement of thought. Thought itself is very limited. So can a human being, you or I or any of us, can we live without the movement of thought, which is the essence of the self?

Suppose the speaker, this person says: yes, it is possible, I know it is possible, then what? What value has it to you? Either you accept it; or you say: don't be silly, and walk away, as it is not possible, and you leave it. But if you want to inquire and say: look, is it possible?—let's find out, not as an idea, but as an actuality in daily life.

G. Narayan: Dr. R, we have been talking in this context of the value of Buddhist meditation, preparation, practice, mindfulness. What is the value of all those things that are mentioned in the Buddhist literature, which is practiced as a very important thing in relation to the ending of thought?

K: Sir, I hope you don't think me impudent or irreverent to what the Buddha said. I personally haven't read all these things. I don't want to read a thing about all this. They may be correct or not correct, they may be under illusion or not under illusion, they may have been put together by disciples, and what the disciples do with their gurus is appalling—twist everything.

So I say: look, I don't want to start with somebody telling me what to do, or what to think. I have no authority. I say: look, as a human being—suffering, going through agonies, sex and mischief, and terror, and all the rest of it—in inquiring into all that I come to the point, which is thought. That's all.

I don't have to know all the literature in the world, which will only condition further thinking. So forgive me for putting it that way: I brush all that aside. We have done this—Christians, I have met Christians, Benedictine monks, Jesuits, great scholars, always quoting, quoting, quoting, believing this is so, this is not so. You understand sir? I hope you don't think I am irreverent.

You see, I only start with what is a fact, for me. What is a fact, not according to some philosophers and religious teachers and priests, a fact: I suffer, I have fear, I have sexual demands. How am I to deal with all these tremendously complex things which make my life?—and I am so utterly miserable, unhappy. From there I start, not from what somebody said, that means nothing. I am not belittling—forgive me—the Buddha, I wouldn't.

WR: That, I know; I know you have the highest respect for the Buddha. But we have the same attitude, and I want to examine it with you. That is why I put the question.

K: No, sir, not quite, sir, forgive me for saying so, not quite. I start with something which is common to all of us. Not according to the Buddha, not according to some Christian God or Hindu or some group, to me all that is totally irrelevant. They have no place because I suffer; I want to find out to end it.

I see the root of all this confusion, uncertainty, insecurity, travail, effort, the root of this is the self, the 'me'. Now is it possible to be free of the 'me,' which produces all this chaos, both outwardly, politically, religiously, economically, and all the rest of it, and also inwardly, this constant struggle, constant battle, constant effort? I am asking, can thought end? So thought has no future—that which ends then has a totally different beginning, not the beginning of the 'me', ending and picking up again later.

Can this thought end? The priest comes along and says: yes it can end, only identify yourself with Christ, with the Buddha—you follow? Identify, forget yourself. Some people have said, suppress it, identify the self with the highest, which is still the movement of thought. Some people have said, burn out all the senses. They have done it: fasting, do everything for this thing.

Somebody like me comes along and says: effort is the very essence of the self. Do we understand that? Or has it become an idea, and we carry that idea out? A person like me says: effort of any kind only strengthens the self. Now how do you receive that statement? When you eat, you are eating because you are hungry. The stomach receives the food, there is no idea of receiving the food. So can you listen—listen—without the idea of receiving, or accepting, or denying, or arguing, just listen to a statement? It may be false, it may be true, but just listen to it. Can you do it?

After carefully explaining the mood of thought which identifies itself with the form, with the name, with this and that and the other thing—after explaining very carefully, it is said that thought is the very root of the self. Now how do we receive, listen to the truth of that fact, that thought is the root of the self? Is it an idea, a conclusion, or is it an absolute, irrevocable fact?

WR: If you ask me, it is a fact. You see, I listen to it, receive it. I see it.

K: Are you listening as a Buddhist—forgive me for putting it that way?

WR: I don't know.

K: No, you must know.

WR: I am not identifying anything at all. I am not listening to you as a Buddhist or a non-Buddhist.

K: I am asking you, sir, are you listening as a Buddhist? Are you listening as a person who has read a great deal about the Buddha and about what the Buddha has said, and therefore you are comparing and therefore you have gone away from listening? So, are you listening? I am not being personal, sir; forgive me.

WR: Oh, you can be quite free with me—I won't misunderstand you and you won't misunderstand me.

K: No, no. I don't mind you misunderstanding me at all. I can correct it. Are you listening to the idea, to the words, and the implications of those words, or are you listening without any sense of verbal comprehension, which you have gone through quickly, and you say: yes, I see the absolute truth of that?

WR: That is what I said.

K: Do you?

WR: Yes.

K: No, sir. Then it is finished. It is like seeing something tremendously dangerous, it is over, you don't touch it. I wonder if you see it.
When you say something to me about what the Buddha has said, I listen. I say, he is just quoting from what Buddha has said, but he is not saying something I want to know. He is telling me about the Buddha, but I want to know what you think, not what Buddha thought, because then we are establishing a relationship between you and me, and not between you, Buddha, and me. I wonder if you see that.

26

David Bohm: It seems to me this question of identification is the main one, it is very subtle, in spite of all that you have said, identification still goes on.

K: Of course.

DB: It seems to be built into us.

Questioner: And this raises a question whether that identification can be ended—if I understood rightly.

DB: Identification prevented listening freely, openly, because one listens through the identification.

K: What does identification mean? Why do human beings identify themselves with something: my car, my house, my wife, my children, my country, my god, my—you follow? Why?

Q: To be something, perhaps.

K: Let's inquire why. I identify not only with outward things, but also inwardly with my experience. I identify with experience and say: this is *my* experience. Why do human beings go through this all the time?

DB: At one stage you said we identify with our sensations, for example, our senses, and this seems very powerful. What would it be not to identify with our sensations?

K: When I listen, am I listening to identify myself with the fact, or is there no identification at all and therefore listening with a totally different ear? Am I hearing with the ears of my hearing, or am I hearing with total attention? Am I listening with total attention or is my mind wandering off and saying, "Oh my goodness, this is rather boring"?
Can I attend so completely that there is only the act of listening and nothing else, no identification, no saying: yes,

that is a good idea, bad idea, that's true, that's false—which are all processes of identification—but without any of those movements, can I listen?

When I do so listen, then what? The truth that thought is the essence of the self, and the self creates all this misery, is finished. I don't have to meditate, I don't have to practice; it is over when I see the danger of these things. Can we listen so completely that there is the absence of the self? And one says: can I see, observe something without the self—which is, my country, I love that sky, it is a beautiful sky, and all the rest of that. The ending of thought, which is the ending, or cutting at the very, very root of the self—a bad simile, but take that—when there is such active, attentive, nonidentifying attention, then does the self exist?

I need a suit, why should there be identification in getting a suit? I get it; there is getting it. So the active listening implies listening to the senses, to my taste, the whole sensory movement. I mean, you can't stop the senses, then you would be paralyzed. But the moment I say, "That's a marvelous taste, I must have more of that"—begins the whole identification.

DB: It seems to me that that is the general condition of mankind, to be identifying with the senses. Now how are we going to change that?

K: That is the whole problem sir. Mankind had been educated, conditioned for millennia, to identify with everything: my guru, my house, my god, my country, my king, my queen, and all the horror that goes on.

DB: You see, with each one of those there is a sensation.

K: It is a sensation, which you call experience. When there is the ending of the self, what takes place? Not at the end of my life, not when the brain becomes deteriorated; when the brain is very, very active, quiet, alive, what then takes place, when the self is not? Now, how can you find out, sir?

Say, X has ended the self completely, not picks it up in the future, another day, but ends it completely; he says: yes, there is a totally different activity which is not the self. What good is that to me, or to any of us? He says: yes, it can end, it is a different world altogether, different dimension: not a sensory dimension, not an intellectual projected dimension, something totally different. I say he must be either a cuckoo, a charlatan, or a hypocrite; but I want to find out, not because he says so, but I want to find out.

Can I, as a human being—living in this tremendously ugly, brutal, violent world, economically, socially, morally, and all the rest of it—live without the self? I want to find out. And I want to find out not as an idea; I want to do it, it's my passion. Then I begin to inquire: why is there identification with the form, with the name?—it is not very important whether you are K or W or Y. So you examine this very, very carefully, not to identify yourself with anything, with sensation, with ideas, with a country, with an experience. You understand sir? Can you do it? Not vaguely and occasionally, but with passion, with intensity to find out.

Then what place has thought? You understand, sir? What place has thought? Has it any place at all? Obviously, when I am talking I am using words, the words are associated with memory and so on and so on, so there is thinking there—not with me, there is very little thinking as I am talking, don't let's go into that.

So thought has a place. When I have to catch a train, when I have to go to the dentist, when I go to do something, thought has its place. But it has no place psychologically as when there is the identifying process taking place. Right? I wonder if you see.

DB: You are saying it is identification that makes thought do all the wrong things.

K: That's right. Identification has made thought do the wrong things.

DB: It would be all right otherwise.

K: Otherwise thought has its place.

DB: But when you say no identification, you mean the self is empty, that it has no content, doesn't it?

K: There are only sensations.

DB: Sensations, but they are not identified. They are just going on, do you mean?

K: Yes, sensations are going on.

DB: Outside or inside.

K: Inside.

GN: And you are also implying there is no slipping back.

K: Of course not. When you see something most dangerous, you don't slip back or go forward; it is dangerous. Sir, then is that death? That is the question we began with. Is there a living with the sensations fully awakened?—they are awakened, they are alive, but the nonidentifying with sensation deprives, wipes away the self. We said that. Is it possible to live a daily life with death, which is the ending of the self? The moment you have an insight, it is finished.

DB: Would you say the insight transforms the person?

K: The insight transforms not only the state of the mind, but the brain cells themselves undergo a change.

DB: Therefore the brain cells being in a different state behave differently; it is not necessary to repeat the insight.

K: Either it is so, or it is not so. I am left with this

now—I am left with the question of what is death. Is the ending of the self death?—death in the ordinary accepted sense of the word. It is not, obviously, because the blood is circulating, the brain is working, the heart is pumping, and all the rest of it.

DB: It is still alive.

K: It is alive but the self is nonexistent because there is no identification of any kind. This is a tremendous thing. Nonidentification with anything, with experience, with belief, with a country, with ideas, with ideals, wife, husband, love, no identification at all.

Is that death? People who call that death say: my god, if I don't identify myself with my something or other, why I am nothing. So they are afraid of being nothing—then identify. But nothingness is not a thing—you understand, sir, not a thing—therefore it is quite a different state of mind. Now that is death while there is living, breathing, sensations, the heart beating, the blood circulating, the brain active, undamaged. But our brains are damaged.

DB: Can this damage be healed? Is it possible to heal the damage?

K: Insight, that is what I want to get at. Our brains are damaged. For thousands of years we have been hurt psychologically, inwardly, and that hurt is part of our brain cells, remembered hurts: the propaganda for two thousand years that I am a Christian, that I believe in Jesus Christ, which is a hurt; or I am a Buddhist—you follow, sir—that is a hurt. So our brains are damaged. To heal that damage is to listen very carefully, to listen, and in the listening to have an insight into what is being said, and therefore there is immediately a change in the brain cells. Therefore there is no identification, complete and total.

Do you see the truth that identification is the root of the self, with thought and all the rest of it? That is an absolute

31

fact, like a cobra, like a dangerous animal, like a precipice, like taking deadly poison. So there is no identification, absolutely, when you see the danger.

Then what is my relationship to the world, to nature, to my woman, man, child? When there is no identification, is there indifference, callousness, brutality? Do I say, "I don't identify," and put my nose in the air?

I am asking, sir, is this nonidentification an ideal, a belief, an idea which I am going to live with and therefore my relationship to the dog, to the wife, to the husband, to the girl, or whatever it is becomes very superficial, casual. It is only when identification is absolutely cut out of one's life that there is no callousness, because then relationship is real.[13]

I THINK IT IS VERY IMPORTANT to understand the relationship between you and the speaker; because if that relationship is not clearly understood, it will lead to a great deal of confusion.

The speaker is not important at all, he is merely the voice, the telephone; but what is said, when one is in the process of learning, has an immense significance. If you give importance to the speaker as a teacher, you are merely creating a following, and thereby you are destroying yourself as well as what is being said. Both the follower and the teacher are a detriment to the process of learning; and when one is intent on learning, there is neither the teacher nor the follower.

I think it is also important to understand that I am not talking to you as an individual who is opposed to society, or as one who belongs to this or that group. To me there is only the human being, whether he lives in India, in America, in Russia, in Germany, or anywhere else. I am not talking to you as an Indian with a particular system of beliefs, but together we are endeavoring to find out what this whole process of living is all about.

This is our earth, it is not the Englishman's or the Russian's, the American's or the Indian's; it is the earth on which we live, you and I. It does not belong to the communist or the capitalist, the Christian or the Hindu. It is our earth, to be lived on extensively, widely, and deeply; but that living is denied when you are a nationalist, when you belong to a party or an organized religion. Please believe me, these are the very things that are destroying human beings.

Nationalism is a curse. To call oneself a Hindu or a Christian is also a curse, because it divides us. We are human beings, not members of a sect or functionaries in a system. But the politician, the man who is committed to a conclusion or a system in which he has a vested interest, will exploit each one of us through our nationalism, through our vanity and emotionalism, just as the priest exploits us in the name of so-called religion.

In considering these things together, I think it is very important for each one of us to understand that hearing is one thing, and listening, which brings action, is quite another. You may superficially agree when you hear it said that nationalism, with all its emotionalism and vested interest, leads to exploitation and the setting of man against man; but to really free your mind from the pettiness of nationalism is another matter.

To be free, not only from nationalism, but also from all the conclusions of organized religions and political systems, is essential if the mind is to be young, fresh, innocent, that is, in a state of revolution; and it is only such a mind that can create a new world—not the politicians, who are dead, nor the priests, who are caught in their own religious systems.

Fortunately or unfortunately for yourself, you have heard something which is true; and if you merely hear it and are not actively disturbed so that your mind begins to free itself from all the things which are making it narrow and crooked, then the truth you have heard will become a poison. Surely, truth becomes a poison, if it is heard and does not act in the mind— like the festering of a wound. But to discover for oneself what is true and what is false, and to see the truth in the false, is to let that truth operate and bring forth its own action.

It is obviously of the greatest importance that as individual human beings we understand for ourselves this whole process of living. Living is not just a matter of function and status, and if we are content to be mere functionaries with a certain status, we become mechanical, and then life passes us by. It seems to me that if one does not really participate in life, take to one's heart the fullness of life, then the mind becomes petty, narrow, full of the dogmatic beliefs which are now destroying human beings.

I do not know if you have ever gone deeply within yourself. To do that, surely, you must put aside all explanations, all conclusions about yourself, all the knowledge you have acquired about the self. Only a free mind is capable of inquiring, not a mind that is tethered to some conclusion, belief, or dogma.

If you have ever inquired very deeply into yourself, you are bound to have come upon that state which we call loneliness, a sense of complete isolation, of not being related. As a human being, you must at some time have felt that desperate, agonizing, despairing sense of isolation, from which consciously or unconsciously we are always running away. In our flight from the reality of that extraordinary sense of loneliness, we are driven, are we not, by a deep urge that is everlastingly seeking fulfillment through books, through music, through work and activity, through position, power, prestige.

If at any time you have felt that sense of utter loneliness; or if you have ever consciously, deliberately allowed yourself to be aware of it, you will know that you immediately want to run away, to escape from it. You go to the temple, worship a god, plunge into perpetual activity, talk everlastingly, explain things away, or turn on the radio. We all do this, as we well know if we are at all conscious of ourselves.

Now, to realize that escape in any form will never satisfy this deep urge for self-fulfillment, to see that it is insatiable, a bottomless pit, you must be aware of it totally, which means that you must see the truth that escapes have no reality. You may escape through God or through drink, but they are both the same; one is nòt more sacred than the other.

You have to understand this hidden urge and go beyond it; and you cannot understand and go beyond it if you have not tasted that extraordinary loneliness, that darkness which has no way out, no hope. Hope comes into being when there is despair. A mind is in despair only because it is frustrated in its hope. To understand this deep urge, this hidden want, you must perceive it totally, as you might perceive a tree or a lovely flower. Then you can go beyond it; and once beyond it, you will find there is a complete aloneness which is entirely different from being lonely. But you cannot discover that state of complete aloneness without understanding the deep urge to fulfill yourself, to escape from loneliness.

All this may sound unusual, unreal, and perhaps you will say, "What has this got to do with our daily living?" I think it is intimately related to your daily living, because your daily living is a misery of frustration; there is an everlasting striving to be, to become something, which is the real outcome of this deep urge, this hidden want. On the surface you may practice discipline, control your mind, meditate, talk about peace, or what you will, but it is all nonsense as long as you do not understand the hidden want that is driving you.

That state of aloneness is essential, because our minds are worn out with constant effort. What is your life? You are constantly trying to be this and not to be that, striving ever-lastingly to become famous, to get a better job, to be more efficient; you are making endless effort, are you not? I wonder if you have ever noticed what a miserable existence we have, always striving to be something, to be good, to be nonviolent, ceaselessly talking about peace while indulging in political emotionalism and preparing for war. Our life is one of strife, turmoil, travail, and a mind in that condition can never be fresh, young, new.

Surely, seeing all this, one must have asked oneself whether such effort is necessary to live in this world. There may be a different way of living altogether, a way of living without effort—not at the lowest level, like a cow, nor like a human being who is forever doing what he likes, but at the highest level, a level where there is no effort.

But you cannot say: "How am I to realize that state of mind in which there is no effort?" because the very desire to acquire that state is another form of attachment, and all attachment is to things that are dying, or dead. You are attached to the dead, not to the living. You are attached, not to your wife who is a living human being, but to the wife of pleasurable memory. You cannot be attached to the living, moving river; you are attached to the pleasure of having seen that river, which is a memory, a dead thing.

There is a way of living which is completely effortless. Please, I am not asking you to accept this. It has nothing to do with acceptance or denial. You simply don't know it. All you know is effort, strife; you are perpetually driving yourself to be or not to be something, and your aggressive pursuit of your own ambitions, with its tensions and contradictions, is the outcome of this hidden want.

You cannot remove this hidden want by mesmerizing yourself. You have to look at it; and you cannot look at it as long as you are escaping. You can look at it only when you come to it completely without fear because it is the fact. Don't dictate what the fact should be; let the fact tell you what it is. Most of us come to the fact with an opinion about the fact, with knowledge, with belief, which is an immature, a childish thing to do. You must come to the fact with innocence, with a fullness of heart, which is humility. Then the fact will tell you what it is.

This hidden want is extraordinarily deep and subtle; but if you are able to look at it without any opinion, without any fear, then you will discover that you can go beyond its darkness to a state in which the mind is totally alone and therefore no longer the result of influence. This aloneness is the state of attention.

In this aloneness, which is the state of attention, there is no shadow of concentration. Being alone, uninfluenced, not caught in opinion, the mind is completely attentive; it is motionless, silent, utterly still. But you cannot make the mind still. You can mesmerize the mind by repeating certain phrases, or quiet it by prayer, but that is not stillness, that is death. It is like putting the mind in a straight-jacket to hold it still—and therefore the mind decays.

What is essential is to understand this deep, hidden want, which is always changing—and that is the beauty of it. You think you have understood it, only to find that it has moved somewhere else. So one has to pursue this hidden want down all the dark corridors of the mind. Then there comes that aloneness which is attention, and which is really a motionless state. I am not using that word *motionless* in opposition to activity. A mind that is motionless, still, is not a dead mind. It is an active mind, it is activity itself, because it is still, and only such a mind is creative.[14]

Emotion

FEAR

WHAT BRINGS FREEDOM FROM FEAR—and I assure you the freedom is complete—is to be aware of fear without the word, without trying to deny or escape from fear, without wanting to be in some other state. If with complete attention you are aware of the fact that there is fear, then you will find that the observer and the observed are one, there is no division between them. There is no observer who says, "I am afraid"; there is only fear without the word which indicates that state. The mind is no longer escaping, no longer seeking to get rid of fear, no longer trying to find the cause, and therefore it is no longer a slave to words. There is only a movement of learning which is the outcome of innocence, and an innocent mind has no fear.[15]

HAVE YOU ANY KIND OF FEAR, physical or psychological? If one has psychological fears, how do you deal with them? If I am afraid that I shall lose my position, my prestige, I depend on the audience, on you, to bolster me up. I depend on you to give me vitality by talking. And I am afraid if I grow older, become senile, I will be faced with nothing and I am afraid. Or I am afraid that I depend on you. Dependency makes me attached to you, and I am afraid to lose you. I am afraid I have done something in the past, which I regret or I am ashamed of, and I don't want you to know, so I am afraid of that, of your knowing it. And I feel guilty. Or I feel terribly anxious—about death, living, what people say, what people don't say, how they look at me, the deep sense of foreboding, anxiety, a sense of inferiority, living a life that has no meaning.

Out of my anxiety I seek some assurance from somebody in human relationship, or I seek a sense of security in a certain belief, in an ideology, in God, and so on. And also I am afraid that I shan't be able to do everything I want to do in this life. I haven't the capacity, or the intelligence, but I am tremendously ambitious to achieve something. And so I am frightened of that too. And, of course, I am afraid of death, and I am afraid of being lonely, not being loved; and so I want to establish a relationship with another in which this fear doesn't exist, this anxiety, this sense of loneliness, this separation. And also I am afraid of the dark—the innumerable neurotic fears that one has.

Now what is this fear? Why is there this fear? Is it based on not being hurt, not to be hurt? Or is it that one wants complete security and not being able to find it, physically, emotionally, psychologically, intellectually, not being able to find this sense of complete safety, security, protection, one becomes terribly anxious about living?

One of our major problems is fear, whether we are aware of it or not. Whether we run away from it, or try to overcome it, try to withstand it, develop courage and so on, there is still fear. Is the mind so delicate, so sensitive, that it doesn't want to be hurt, from childhood on. And so, not wanting to be hurt, one builds a wall, one is very shy, or aggressive. Before you attack I am ready to attack you, verbally, with thought, because I am so sensitive, I have been hurt so much in my life, in my childhood. In the office, in the factory, everybody treads on each other's toes, and I don't want to be hurt. Is that one of the reasons why fear exists? You have been hurt, haven't you? And out of that hurt we do all kinds of things, we resist a great deal, we don't want to be disturbed. Out of that feeling of hurt we cling to something that we hope will protect us. And therefore I become aggressive towards anything that attacks that which I am holding on to as protection.

What is it that you as a human being are frightened of? Is it a physical fear? Fear not to have any more physical pain? Or a psychological fear of danger? Of uncertainty? Of being further hurt? Of not being able to find total complete security, certainty? Fear of not wanting to be dominated and yet we are dominated? So what is it that you, as a human being, are frightened of? Are you aware of your fear?[16]

FEAR, PLEASURE, AND SORROW have existed from time beyond thought. Man has always had these three factors in life: fear, the pursuit of pleasure, and sorrow. And apparently man has not gone beyond that. We have tried every method, every system that you can think of. We have tried to suppress it, tried to escape from it, tried to invent a god and surrender all to that invention. But that has not worked either. So we must find out whether sorrow can end, and understand the nature of sorrow, the cause of sorrow. Is the cause different from fear? Is the cause different from pleasure—pleasure of achievement, pleasure of possession, pleasure of having great power, pleasure of talent, pleasure of wealth?

So let us find out whether sorrow and fear can ever end? The pursuit of pleasure is infinite, endless, not only of sexual pleasure, but also the pleasure of becoming something, the pleasure of achievement, the pleasure of being attached to somebody, whether that attachment is to a person, to an idea, or to a conclusion. And while you are pursuing that pleasure, there is always the shadow of fear with it. And where there is fear, there is sorrow. Fear is not separate, they are all together; they are all interrelated and one must deal with them all wholly, not separately. You must approach this whole thing wholly, not fragmentarily; if you approach it fragmentarily you will never solve it.

Greed, pain, sorrow is a movement of life, a whole move-ment of life, not something different from life. This *is* our daily life. And to find out whether there is an end to all this—to misery, to conflict, pain, sorrow, and fear—one must be able to perceive them, one must be able to be aware of them. So we must understand what perception is, how to look at all this. Is the poverty, the loneliness, the anxiety, the uncertainty, the suffering different from the observer or is all that the observer?

We have separated the 'me' who is the observer from that which he is observing. I say I am suffering, and I say to myself that suffering must end, and to end it I must suppress it, I must escape from it, I must follow a certain system. So I am different from fear, from pleasure, from pain, sorrow. Are you different from all that? You may think that there is something in you which is totally different from all that, but if you think that, that is part of your thought, and therefore there is nothing sacred there. Is the observer different from the observed?

Don't make it absurd. You see a tree and when you say, "Am I different from the tree?"—you are, I hope. But when you are angry, envious, brutal, violent, are you not all that? See the importance of this. We have divided the observer from the observed. That means there is a division between that and the other. So there is conflict. You control it, suppress it, fight it, but if you are that, if you are sorrow, if you are fear, if you are pleasure, you are this whole conglomeration. And to realize that fact is a tremendous reality. Therefore, there is no division and therefore there is no conflict. Then the observer is the observed. Then a totally different action takes place, a totally different chemical action takes place.

It is not an intellectual achievement to see the truth of it, not the intellectual concept of the truth but the fact that you are not different from your qualities. You are not different from your anger, jealousy, hatred—you *are* all that. You know what happens when you realize that, not verbally but inwardly? Find out. I won't tell you! You see how your mind works. You are waiting for me to tell you. You don't want to find out. If I tell you then you will say: yes, right or wrong, but you will go on. But find out for yourself the actual truth of it, that the observer is the observed, the watcher is the watched.

When you watch the full moon, that moon is not you, unless you are loony. But you are the whole bundle of your consciousness. The content of your consciousness is what you are, and the content of that consciousness is put together by thought. Now find out, not the ending of thought but how to observe the content. When you observe without the division, then a totally different action takes place. Where there is love, there is no observer, there is no you and the one that you love, there is only that quality of love.[17]

Questioner: If, as you say, fear and pleasure are related, can one remove fear and so enjoy pleasure completely?

Krishnamurti: Lovely, wouldn't it be? Take away all my fears so that I can enjoy myself in my pleasures. Everybody right through the world wants the same thing, some very crudely, some very subtly—to escape fear and hold on to pleasure. Pleasure—you smoke, it is a pleasure, yet there is pain within it because you may get a disease. You have had pleasure, whether as man or woman, sexually or otherwise, comfort and so on; when the other looks away you are jealous, angry, frustrated, mutilated.

Pleasure inevitably brings pain. We are not saying we cannot have pleasure; but see the whole structure and you will know then that joy, real enjoyment, the beauty of enjoyment, the freedom of it, has nothing whatsoever to do with pleasure or therefore with pain or fear. If you see that, the truth of it, then you will understand pleasure and give it its proper place.

Q: Aren't there some fears that are useful at least for survival? For example, I'm very much afraid of jumping from the Empire State building.

K: Surely. When physically you face a danger, the natural response is self-protection. Physical survival—is that fear or is it intelligence? Now we don't apply that same intelligence with regard to fear, the inward fears, the psychological fears. Look at this sir, very simply. The world has divided itself into nationalities and religious groups and political groups. This division is bringing about war, hatred. And that very war is destroying us, though we think through nationalism we shall have security. When one realizes all this, intelligence becomes extraordinarily important. And you know when that intelligence is operating, and it can operate only when there is no fear.[18]

Mary Zimbalist: Sir, there is a subject you have talked about so many, many times but it keeps coming back and back in people's questions and preoccupations, and that is the subject of fear. Do you want to talk about that?

K: It is a rather complicated subject. It really requires a great deal of inquiry because it is so subtle, so varied, and so abstract. And also it is actual too, though we make it into an abstraction. The actuality of fear and the idea of fear, which is the abstraction of fear into an idea. So we must be very clear what we are talking about. The abstraction as an idea of fear, or the actuality of fear. You and I sitting, and all of us sitting here, at this present moment we are not afraid. There is no sense of apprehension, or danger. At this instant there is no fear.

So fear is both an abstraction, as an idea, as a word, and also a fact. First of all let's deal with these two. Why do we generally make an abstraction of things? Why do we see something actual and then turn it into an idea? Is it because the idea is easier to pursue? Or the ideal is our conditioning? Or we are educated to ideas, or in ideas, not educated to deal with facts? Why is this? Why is it that human beings throughout the world deal with abstractions—what should be, what must be, what will happen, and so on, the whole world of ideation and the ideologies, whether it be the communist ideology based on Marx and Lenin, or the capitalists' ideas of so-called free enterprise and so on, or the whole world of religious concepts, beliefs, ideas, and the theologians working these ideas out. Why is it that ideas, ideals, have become so extraordinarily important? From the ancient Greeks, even before the Greeks and so on, ideas prevailed. And even now ideas, ideals, separate man and they bring wars, all kinds. Why do the brains of human beings operate this way?

Is it because they cannot deal with facts directly and so escape subtly into ideations? If one sees ideas are really very divisive factors, they bring friction, they divide communities, nations, sects, religions, and so on—which is, ideas, beliefs, faith, all that is based on thought. And facts, what are facts? What exactly is a fact, not an opinion about a fact, or opinion made into facts.

MZ: What is the fact of fear, sir?

K: I am coming to that. First we must establish the distinction between the idea of fear, the abstraction as the word *fear*, and the actual fear. The actual fear is the fact, not the abstraction of it. If one can move away from the abstraction then we can deal with fact. But if they are both running parallel all the time, then there is a conflict between the two. That is, the idea, the ideology dominating the fact and the fact sometimes dominating the idea.

MZ: Most people would say that the fact of fear is a very painful emotion.

K: So let us look at the fact—that is what I am coming to—the fact of actual fear, and remain with that fact, which requires a great deal of inward discipline.

MZ: Can you describe what 'remaining with the fact of fear' actually is?

K: It is like holding a jewel, an intricate pattern by an artist, who has brought this extraordinary jewel. You look at it, you don't condemn it, you don't say, "How beautiful" and run away with words, but you are looking at this extraordinary thing put together by hand, by cunning fingers and the brain that has brought this. You are watching it, you are looking at it. Turn it around, look at the various sides, the back and the front and the side, and you never let it go.

MZ: Do you mean that you just feel it very acutely, very sensitively, with great care.

K: With care, that is what happens.

MZ: But you feel it because it is an emotion.

K: Of course. You have the feeling of beauty, the feeling of the intricate pattern, and the sparkle, the brightness, and the sparkle of the jewels and so on. So can we deal with the fact of fear and look at it that way, not escape, not say, "Well I don't like fear," get nervous, apprehensive, and suppress it, or control it, or deny it, or move it into another field. If we can do all that, just remain with that fear, fear then becomes an actual fact, which is there, whether you are conscious of it or not, whether you have hidden it very, very deeply, it is still there.

Then we can ask very carefully and hesitantly, what is this fear? Why do human beings, after this tremendous evolution, still live with fear? Is it something that can be operated upon and removed—like a disease, like cancer, or any other dreadful, painful disease? Is it something that can be operated upon? Which means there is an entity who can operate upon it, but that very entity is an abstraction of trying to do something about fear, that entity is unreal. What is factual is fear.

This requires very careful attention not to be caught in this abstraction of the one who says, "I am observing fear," or one who says, "I must put away fear, or control fear," and so on. The one who watches is also the outcome of fear. If this is clear, that the observer—to go back to our old saying—the observer is the observed, the thinker is the thought, the doer is the entity who is doing, there is no division. And so if there is no division—which is an extraordinary fact to realize, a fact, not an idea I must realize, it is an extraordinary fact that there is no division between the observer and the observed—therefore there is no conflict. Conflict exists when there is the observer different from the observed, which is what most of us do and therefore live with perpetual conflict. That is another matter.

So can we look at fear, and in the very act of looking, watching, begin to discover the origin of fear, the beginning of it, the cause of it? Because the very act of looking at it is to see how it came about. Not that we analyze fear, because the analyzer is the analyzed; not that we dissect fear, but very close, delicate watching reveals the content of fear, the content being the origin, the beginning, the causation. Where there is a cause there is an end. The cause can never be different from the result. In the observation, in the watching, the causation is revealed.

MZ: Sir, the causation that you are speaking of is presumably not an individual fear, a particular fear? You are speaking of the causation of fear itself.

K: Fear itself, not the various forms of fear. See how we break up fear. That's part of our tradition, to bring about a fragmentation of fear, therefore be concerned only with one type of fear, not the whole tree of fear; not a particular branch, or a particular leaf of fear but the whole nature, the structure, the quality of fear. And in observing that very closely, watching it, in the very watching there is the revelation of the causation—not you analyze to find out the cause but the very watching is showing the causation, which is time and thought. Of course. That is simple when you put it that way. Everybody would accept it is time and thought. If there were no time and thought, there would be no fear.

MZ: Well, could you enlarge a little bit on that, because most people think that there is something. That there is— how can I put it—they don't see that there is no future, they think "I am afraid now" from a cause, they don't see the factor of time involved.

K: I think it is fairly simple. If there were no time, or if there was no saying: I am afraid because I have done something in the past, or I have had pain in the past, or somebody has hurt me, and I don't want to be hurt anymore—all that is the past, the background, which is time. And the future, that is: I am this now, I will die, or I might lose my job, or my wife will be angry with me and so on.

There is this past and the future, and we are caught in between the two.

That is, the past has its relationship with the future, the future is not something separate from the past, it is a movement of modification from the past to the future, to tomorrow. That is time, this movement of the past, which is: the past as I have been, and the future, I will be, which is this constant becoming. And that too is another complex problem which we won't touch for the moment. That may be the causation of fear, the becoming.

So time is a factor, is a basic factor of fear. There is no question about it. I have a job now, I have money now, I have a shelter over my head, but tomorrow or many hundred tomorrows might deprive me of all that, some accident, some fire, some lack of insurance, and so on. All that is a time factor. Not the ending of time, but see the factor that fear is part of time; not say, "Can I end time?"—that is a silly question. Sorry to use the word *silly*.

Also thought is a factor of fear—thought: I have been, I am, but I may not be. The factor of thought, which is limited, which is another matter. Thought is limited because it is based on knowledge, knowledge is always accumulative and that which is being added to is always limited, so knowledge is limited, so thought is limited because thought is based on knowledge, memory, and so on.

Thought and time are the central factors of fear. Thought is not separate from time. They are one, they are not divorced, they are not separate. These are the facts. This is the causation of fear. Now that is a fact, not an idea, not an abstraction, that thought and time is the cause of fear, not *are*—it is singular.

So a man then asks: how do I stop time and thought? Because his intention, his desire, his longing is to be free from fear. And so he is caught in his own desire to be free, but he is not watching the causation very carefully. Watching implies a state of the brain in which there is no movement. It is like watching a bird, and if you watch the bird very closely—as we watched this morning that dove on the windowsill—you watch all the feathers, the red eyes, the sparkle in the eyes, the beak, the shape of its head, the wings. You watch very carefully, and that which you watch very carefully reveals not only the causation but the ending of the thing you are watching.

This watching is really most extraordinarily important. We may ask how to end thought, or how to be free from fear, or what time means, and all the complications of that, but when we are watching fear without any abstraction, it is the actual now because the now contains all time; the present holds the past, the future, and the present. In that quality of the now, can we listen very carefully, not only with the hearing of the ear, but listen to the word and go beyond the word to see the actual nature of fear. You are then not reading about fear; in watching it becomes extraordinarily beautiful, sensitive, alive.

All this requires an extraordinary quality of attention, because in attention there is no activity of the self. The self-interest in our life is the cause of fear. This sense of me and my concern, my happiness, my success, my failure, my achievement, I am this, I am not—this whole self-centered observation with all its expressions of fear, agonies, depression, pain, anxiety, aspiration, and sorrow all that is self-interest, whether in the name of God, in the name of prayer, in the name of faith, it is self-interest. Where there is self-interest there must be fear, and all the consequences of fear.

Then one asks again: Is it possible to live in this world where self-interest is predominant—whether it is in the totalitarian world, with its search for power and holding power, or the capitalist world with its own power, self-interest is dominant. Whether it is in the religious hierarchical Catholic world or in every religious world, self-interest is dominant and therefore they are perpetuating fear—though they talk about living with *pacem in terris,* which is peace on earth, they really don't mean it, because self-interest with the desire for power, position, for its fulfillment and so on, is the factor that is destroying not only the world but destroying our own extraordinary capacity of the brain.

The brain has extraordinary capacity, as is shown in the technological world, the extraordinary things they are doing. And we never apply that same immense capacity inwardly to be free of fear, to end sorrow, to know what love is, and compassion with its intelligence. We never search, explore that field, we are caught by the world with all its misery.[19]

NOW, WHAT IS FEAR? We are not dealing with ideas, with words. We are dealing with life, with the things which are happening inside and outside, which needs a very clear, sharp mind, a precise mind; you cannot be sentimental, emotional about all these things. To understand fear, you need clarity—clarity not of something that you will get, but the clarity that comes when you understand that the fact is infinitely more important than any idea. So, what is fear—not fear of something? Is there such a thing as fear per se, in itself, or is fear always related to something? And is there fear?

I will take death for the moment. You can supply your own example. Is there fear if there is no thought—that is, if there is no time? Most people are afraid of death. However much they might have rationalized it, whatever their beliefs may be, there is the fear of death. That fear is caused by time—not by death, but by time—time being the interval between now and what is going to happen, which is the process of thinking, which brings about the fear of the unknown. Is it the fear of the unknown or the fear of leaving the things that we know?

We are afraid of death. We are not talking of death or what happens after death; we are talking of fear in relation to death. I say: is that fear caused by the thing which I do not know? Obviously I do not know about death. I can know about it, but that is not the point now. I can investigate, discover the whole beauty or the ugliness or the terror, the extraordinary state death must be.

Is the fear in relation to death caused by death—which means facing the unknown? Or is it caused by the things which I know are going to be taken away from me? The fear is of the things taken away from me, the 'me' disappearing into oblivion. And so I begin to protect myself with all the things that I know and live in them more strongly, cling to them much more, than become aware of the unknown.

What is it I am afraid of? Not facing the unknown, but facing something which may happen to me when I am taken away from all the things that are held dear, which are close to me—that is what I am afraid of, not of death. What is it that I have—factually, not theoretically? I do not know if you have ever asked yourself a fundamental question to find out what you are.

Have you ever asked it, and have you found an answer? Is there an answer? If there is an answer, it is not in terms of what you already know. But what you know is the past, and the past is time; and the time is not 'you'. The 'you' is changing. The thing that is alive never engenders fear. It is the thing that is past, or the thing that should be, that breeds fear.

We are caught in words. Why has the word become important and not the thing? Because you can play with ideas, you cannot play with the fact. We are slaves to words. So, in understanding fear, there must be an awareness of the word and all the content of the word—which means, the mind has to be free of words. To be free of the word is an extraordinary state. Being aware of the symbol, the word, the name, is awareness of the fact at a different dimension—if I can use that word.

Now I am aware of the fact of fear through the word, and I know why the word comes into being. It is an escape, it is tradition, it is the background in which I have been brought up, to deny fear and to develop courage—the opposite—and all the rest of it. And when I understand the whole implication of the word, then there is an awareness of the fact, which is entirely different.[20]

YOU KNOW, WHAT THIS WORLD NEEDS is not politicians, or more engineers, but free human beings. Engineers and scientists may be necessary, but it seems to me that what the world needs is human beings who are free, who are creative, who have no fear; and most of us are ridden with fear. If you can go profoundly into fear and really understand it, you will come out with innocence, so that your mind is clear. That is what we need, and that is why it is very important to understand how to look at a fact, how to look at your fear. That is the whole problem—not how to get rid of fear, not how to be courageous, not what to do about fear, but to be fully with the fact.

You want to be fully, totally with the wave of pleasure, don't you? And you are. When you are in the moment of pleasure, there is no condemnation, no justification, no denial. There is no factor of time at the moment of experiencing pleasure; physically, sensually, your whole being vibrates with it. Isn't that so? When you are in the moment of experiencing, there is no time, is there? When you are intensely angry, or when you are full of lust, there is no time. Time comes in, thought comes in only after the moment of experiencing; and then you say, "By Jove, how nice," or "How terrible." If it was nice, you want more of it; if it was terrible, fearful, you want to avoid it; therefore you begin to explain, to justify, to condemn, and these are the factors of time which prevent you from looking at the fact.

Now, have you ever faced fear? Please listen to the question carefully. Have you ever looked at fear? Or, in the moment of being aware of fear, are you already in a state of flight from the fact? I will go into it a little bit, and you will see what I mean.

We name, we give a term to our various feelings, don't we? In saying, "I am angry," we have given a term, a name, a label to a particular feeling. Now, please watch your own minds very clearly. When you have a feeling, you name that feeling, you call it anger, lust, love, pleasure. Don't you? And this naming of the feeling is a process of intellection which prevents you from looking at the fact, that is, at the feeling.

When you see a bird and say to yourself that it is a parrot, or a pigeon, or a crow, you are not looking at the bird. You have already ceased to look at the fact, because the word *parrot* or *pigeon* or *crow* has come between you and the fact.

53

This is not some difficult intellectual feat, but a process of the mind that must be understood. If you would go into the problem of fear, or the problem of authority, or the problem of pleasure, or the problem of love, you must see that naming, giving a label, prevents you from looking at the fact. Do you understand?

You see a flower and you call it a rose, and the moment you have thus given it a name, your mind is distracted; you are not giving your full attention to the flower. So, naming, terming, verbalizing, symbolizing prevents total attention towards the fact.

Now, can the mind—which is addicted to symbols and whose very nature it is to verbalize—stop verbalizing, and look at the fact? Don't say, "How am I to do it?" but put the question to yourself. I have a feeling, and I call it fear. By giving it a name I have related it to the past; so memory, the word, the symbol, is preventing me from looking at the fact. Now, can the mind—which in its very thought process verbalizes, gives names—look at the fact without naming it?

You have to find this out for yourselves; I cannot tell you. If I tell you and you do it, you will be following, and you won't be free of fear. What matters is that you should be totally free of fear, and not be half-dead human beings—corrupt, miserable people who are everlastingly afraid of their own shadow.

To understand this problem of fear, you have to go into it most profoundly, because fear is not merely on the surface of the mind. Fear is not just being afraid of your neighbor, or of losing a job; it is much deeper than that, and to understand it requires deep penetration. To penetrate deeply you need a very sharp mind; and the mind is not made sharp by mere argumentation or avoidance. One has to go into the problem step by step, and that is why it is very important to comprehend this whole process of naming. When you name a whole group of people by calling them Moslems, or what you will, you have got rid of them; you don't have to look at them as individuals, so the name, the word has prevented you from being a human being in relationship with other human beings. In the same way, when you name a feeling, you are not looking at the feeling, you are not totally with the fact.

There are innumerable forms of escape from fear; but if you escape, run away, fear will follow you everlastingly. To be fundamentally free of fear, you must understand this process of naming and realize that the word is never the thing. The mind must be capable of separating the word from the feeling, and must not let the word interfere with direct perception of the feeling, which is the fact.

When you have gone so far, penetrated so deeply, you will discover there is buried in the unconscious, in the obscure recesses of the mind, a sense of complete loneliness, of isolation, which is the fundamental cause of fear. And again, if you avoid it, if you escape from it, saying it is too fearful, if you do not go into it without giving it a name, you will never go beyond it. The mind has to come face to face with the fact of complete inward loneliness, and not allow itself to do anything about that fact.

That extraordinary thing called loneliness is the very essence of the self, the 'me', with all its chicaneries, its cunningness, its substitutions, its web of words in which the mind is caught. Only when the mind is capable of going beyond that ultimate loneliness is there freedom—the absolute freedom from fear. And only then will you find out for yourself what is reality, that immeasurable energy which has no beginning and no end. As long as the mind spawns its own fears in terms of time, it is incapable of understanding that which is timeless.[21]

LONELINESS

I DO NOT KNOW IF YOU HAVE EVER BEEN LONELY: when you suddenly realize that you have no relationship with any-body—not an intellectual realization but a factual realization, a thing that is as concrete as this microphone—and you are completely isolated. Every form of thought and emotion is blocked. There is nobody to turn to—the gods, the angels have all gone beyond the clouds and, as the clouds vanish, they have also vanished. You are completely lonely—I will not use the word alone.

Alone has quite a different meaning; alone has beauty. To be alone means something entirely different. And you must be alone. When man frees himself from the social structure of greed, envy, ambition, arrogance, achievement, status—when he frees himself from those, then he is completely alone. That is quite a different thing. Then there is great beauty, the feel-ing of great energy.

But loneliness is not that. Loneliness is this complete sense of being isolated from everything. I do not know if you have felt it. The more you are awake, the more you are questioning, looking, asking, demanding, the more you are aware of it: deep down in your consciousness, at all the levels, you feel com-pletely cut off. And that is one of the great sorrows—not being able to go beyond it, and being caught in that tremendous feel-ing of loneliness with its great energy.

It has got vitality, a drive, an insistence, an ugliness; and we escape from it in every form. Either we are terribly clever, write books about that loneliness, and push aside that loneliness; or we run away, amuse ourselves, and never touch it. And it remains there, hidden; but like a cancerous wound, it is there, waiting. One has to come into contact with it, not verbally but actually.

This loneliness is a form of death. There is dying not only when life comes to an end, but when there is no answer, there is no way out. That is also a form of death: being in the prison of your own self-centered activity endlessly—when you are caught in your own thoughts, in your own agony, in your own superstitions, in your deadly, daily routine of habit. And we will prolong it for another fifty years or more—the same self-centered, brutal activities: ambition, competition, seeking status, position, power, greed, envy.[22]

We LIVE IN THIS PRESSURE OF FAMILIES, of relationship with each other. There is the sexual pressure, the demand over each other, the possessive dependence, attachment, jealousy, anxiety, hatred, and so on. So why do human beings throughout the world live like this? Is it because they are lazy, indifferent, callous that they talk about relationship, and they don't mean a thing by that word? Is it habit, is it tradition, is it that we do not know how to break through this? And perhaps that may be one of the reasons why human beings do accept so easily to live in this conflict.

What do we mean by that word *relationship*? To be related, to be in contact with? When you use the words *in contact with*—not only physically, sexually, but, much more, psychologically—it implies that you are actually in contact psychologically with another. Is that so? Or are you in contact with the image that you have projected about her, the image that thought has created during a thirty-year or forty-year relationship, intimate or not—or during a relationship that lasted for ten days? You create an image about that person; and that image is projected by memory, by experience, by the knowledge that you have accumulated about her or him.

That knowledge is stored in the brain, and that becomes memory, so you are looking at the woman or the man from the knowledge that you have acquired about her. You project that knowledge upon her and you see the image that you have projected, and you think you are in contact with that person, but actually you are only in contact with the image that thought has projected about her or him.[23]

I THINK MOST OF US ARE AWARE SOMETIMES—perhaps only rarely since most of us are so terribly active—that the mind is empty. And, being aware, we are afraid of that emptiness. We have never inquired into that state of emptiness, we have never gone into it deeply, profoundly. We are afraid, and so we wander away from it. We have given it a name, we say it is 'empty', it is 'terrible', it is 'painful'; and that very giving it a name has already created a reaction in the mind, a fear, an avoidance, a running away.

Now, can the mind stop running away, and not give it a name, not give it the significance of a word such as *empty,* about which we have memories of pleasure and pain? Can we look at it, can the mind be aware of that emptiness without naming it, without running away from it, without judging it, but just be with it? Because, then that is the mind. Then there is not an observer looking at it; there is no censor who condemns it; there is only that state of emptiness—with which we are all really quite familiar, but which we are all avoiding, trying to fill it with activity, with worship, with prayer, with knowledge, with every form of illusion and excitement.

But when all the excitement, illusion, fear, running away stops, and you are no longer giving it a name and thereby condemning it, is the observer different then from the thing which is observed? Surely by giving it a name, by condemning it, the mind has created a censor, an observer, outside of itself. But when the mind does not give it a term, a name, condemn it, judge it, then there is no observer, only a state of that thing we have called emptiness.[24]

I WONDER IF WE ARE CONSCIOUS that we do depend psychologically on others? Not that it is necessary or justifiable or wrong, psychologically, to depend on others, but are we, first of all, aware that we are dependent? Most of us are psychologically dependent, not only on people, but on property, on beliefs, on dogmas. Are we at all conscious of that fact? If we know that we do depend on something for our psychological happiness, for our inward stability, security, then we can ask ourselves why.

Why do we psychologically depend on something? Obviously, because in ourselves we are insufficient, poor, empty. In ourselves we are extraordinarily lonely, and it is this loneliness, this emptiness, this extreme inward poverty and self-enclosure that makes us depend on a person, on knowledge, on property, on opinion, and on so many other things which seem necessary to us.

Now, can the mind be fully aware of the fact that it is lonely, insufficient, empty? It is very difficult to be aware, to be fully cognizant of that fact because we are always trying to escape from it; and we do temporarily escape from it through listening to the radio, and other forms of amusement, through going to church, performing rituals, acquiring knowledge, and through dependence on people and on ideas.

To know your own emptiness, you must look at it, but you cannot look at it if your mind is all the time seeking a distraction from the fact that it is empty. And that distraction takes the form of attachment to a person, to the idea of God, to a particular dogma or belief, and so on.

Can the mind stop running away, escaping, and not merely ask how to stop running away? Because the very inquiry into how the mind is to stop escaping becomes another escape. If I know that a certain path does not lead anywhere, I do not walk on that path; there is no question of how not to walk on it. Similarly, if I know that no escape, no amount of running away will ever resolve this loneliness, this inward emptiness, then I stop running, I stop being distracted. Then the mind can look at the fact that it is lonely, and there is no fear. It is in the very process of running away from *what* is that fear arises.

When the mind understands the futility, the utter uselessness of trying to fill its own emptiness through dependence, through knowledge, through belief, then it is capable of looking at it without fear. And can the mind continue to look at that emptiness without any evaluation? When the mind is fully aware that it escapes, runs away from itself, when it realizes the futility of running away and sees that the very process of running away creates fear—when it realizes the truth of that, then it can face *what is*.

Now, what do we mean when we say that we are facing *what is*? Are we facing it, looking at it, if we are always giving a value to it, interpreting it, if we have opinions about it? Surely, opinions, values, interpretations, merely prevent the mind from looking at the fact. If you want to understand the fact, it is no good having an opinion about it. So, can we look, without any evaluation, at the fact of our psychological emptiness, our loneliness, which breeds so many other problems?

I think that is where the difficulty lies—in our incapacity to look at ourselves without judgment, without condemnation, without comparison, because we have all been trained to compare, to judge, to evaluate, to give an opinion. Only when the mind sees the futility of all that, the absurdity of it, is it capable of looking at itself. Then that which we have feared as being lonely, empty, is no longer empty. Then there is no psychological dependence on anything; then love is no longer attachment but something entirely different, and relationship has quite another meaning.

But to find that out for oneself and not merely repeat it verbally, one must understand the process of escape. In the very understanding of escape there is the stopping of escape, and the mind is able to look at itself. In looking at itself, there must be no evaluation, no judgment. Then the fact is important in itself and there is complete attention, without any desire for distraction; therefore, the mind is no longer empty. Complete attention is the good.[25]

I DEPEND ON MY PARENTS when I am young; and as I grow older, I depend on society, on a job, on capacity; and when these fail me, I depend upon faith. There is always a dependence, a faith in something; that dependence sustains me, gives me vitality, energy; and as with all dependences there is always fear, and so I set conflict going.

Or, having no faith, I cultivate consistency, to be constant in my life according to my idea, and that very consistency endangers my self-confidence; the more I am consistent the less I am strong, vital, clear-cut. Self-consistency—to be consistent to a certain form, to a certain action—is what most of us are striving for, which is the cultivation of self-confidence.

Wherever we try, there is always this desire to depend on something to give us strength—on a person, on a particular idea, on a political party, on a system, or on an experience. So there is always a dependence on something to sustain us; and as we depend more and more, there is the cultivation of fear.

Dependence arises because in ourselves we are insufficient, in ourselves we are lonely, in ourselves we are empty. I depend and therefore I cultivate faith; therefore we must have more knowledge; and as we become more and more civilized, more and more learned—materialistic or spiritual—we must have faith or we turn cynics.

For most of us self-confidence is necessary, and for most of us confidence is merely the continuation of an experience or the continuation of knowledge. Does self-confidence ever free the mind from its own conditioning influence? Does this confidence derived through effort bring about freedom or does it merely condition the mind? And is it not possible to free the mind, to remove all dependences? That is, am I capable of being aware of my loneliness, of my complete emptiness, being aware of it without running away from it, and not being consistent through any particular form of knowledge or experience?

That is our problem, is it not? Most of us are running away from ourselves as we are; we cultivate various forms of virtues to help us to run away. We cultivate various forms of confidence, knowledge, experience; we depend on faith. But underneath it all, there is a sense of immense loneliness; and it is only when we are capable of looking at it, living with it, understanding it fully, that there is a possibility of acting without bringing about a series of efforts which condition the mind to a particular action. Please listen to this and you will see it.

All our life we try to be consistent to a particular thought or to a pattern of thought, and the very desire to be consistent creates energy, drive, gives us strength and so narrows down the mind. The mind that is consistent is a very small mind, a petty mind. A small mind has enormous capacity for energy; it derives a great deal of strength from its pettiness, and so our life becomes very small, very limited, very narrow. Can we realize this process of dependence from which we derive strength, in which there is conflict, in which there is fear, envy, jealousy, competition, that constantly narrows down all our efforts so that there is always fear?

Is it not possible to look, to be aware of our loneliness, of our emptiness, and understand it without trying to escape from it? The very understanding of it is not to condemn it, but to be passively aware of it, to listen to the whole content of that loneliness. It means really to go beyond the self, beyond the 'me' and from there act, because our present action is within the confines of the 'me'. It may be enlarged, extended, but it is always the 'me' identifying with a person or an ideal; and that identification gives us a great deal of strength to act, to do, to be, and that identification strengthens the 'me', the 'I', the self in which there is everlasting conflict, everlasting misery; and so all our actions lead to frustration.

Recognizing that, we turn to faith, we turn to God as a source of strength; and that too is the enlargement of the 'me', the strengthening of the 'me', because the 'me' is running away from itself, from that loneliness in itself. When we are capable of facing that loneliness without condemnation or judgment, looking at it, understanding it, hearing the whole content of the 'me', of that loneliness, then only is there a possibility of having strength which is not of the 'me'. Then only is there a possibility of bringing about a different world or a different culture.[26]

DISCONTENT

*H*AVE YOU EVER WONDERED why it is that as people grow older they seem to lose all joy in life, that joyous intimation of something beyond, something of greater significance? Why do so many of us, as we grow into so-called maturity, become dull, insensitive to joy, to beauty, to the open skies and the marvelous earth?

You know, when one asks oneself this question, many explanations spring up in the mind. We are so concerned with ourselves—that is one explanation. We struggle to become somebody, to achieve and maintain a certain position; we have children and other responsibilities, and we have to earn money.

All these external things soon weigh us down, and thereby we lose the joy of living. Look at the older faces around you, see how sad most of them are, how careworn and rather ill, how withdrawn, aloof, and sometimes neurotic, without a smile. Don't you ask yourself why? And even when we do ask why, most of us seem to be satisfied with mere explanations.

Yesterday evening I saw a boat going up the river at full sail, driven by the west wind. It was a large boat, heavily laden with firewood for the town. The sun was setting, and this boat against it; there was no effort, for the wind was doing all the work. Similarly, if each one of us could understand the problem of struggle and conflict, then I think we would be able to live effortlessly, happily, with a smile on our face.

I think it is effort that destroys us, this struggling in which we spend almost every moment of our lives. If you watch the older people around you, you will see that for most of them life is a series of battles with themselves, with

63

their wives or husbands, with their neighbors, with society—and this ceaseless strife dissipates energy.

The man who is joyous, really happy, is not caught up in effort. To be without effort does not mean that you stagnate, that you are dull, stupid; on the contrary, it is only the wise, the extraordinarily intelligent, who are really free of effort, of struggle.

But, you see, when we hear of effortlessness we want to be like that, we want to achieve a state in which we will have no strife, no conflict; so we make that our goal, our ideal, and strive after it; and the moment we do this, we have lost the joy of living. We are again caught up in effort, struggle. The object of struggle varies, but all struggle is essentially the same. One may struggle to bring about social reforms, or to find God, or to create a better relationship between oneself and one's wife or husband, or with one's neighbor; one may sit on the banks of the Ganga, worship at the feet of some guru, and so on. All this is effort, struggle. So what is important is not the object of struggle, but to understand struggle itself.

Now, is it possible for the mind to be, not just casually aware that for the moment it is not struggling, but completely free of struggle all the time so that it discovers a state of joy in which there is no sense of the superior and the inferior?

Our difficulty is that the mind feels inferior, and that is why it struggles to be or become something, or to bridge over its various contradictory desires. But don't let us give explanations of why the mind is full of struggle. Every thinking man knows why there is struggle both within and without.

Our envy, greed, ambition, our competitiveness leading to ruthless efficiency—these are obviously the factors which cause us to struggle, whether in this world or in the world to come. We don't have to study psychological books to know why we struggle; and what is important, surely, is to find out if the mind can be totally free of struggle.

After all, when we struggle, the conflict is between what we are and what we should be or want to be. Now, without giving explanations, can one understand this whole process of struggle so that it comes to an end? Like that boat which was moving with the wind, can the mind be without struggle? Surely, this is the question, and not how to achieve a state in which there is no struggle. The very effort to achieve such a state is itself a process of struggle, therefore that state is never achieved.

But if you observe from moment to moment how the mind gets caught in everlasting struggle—if you just observe the fact without trying to alter it, without trying to force upon the mind a certain state which you call peace—then you will find that the mind spontaneously ceases to struggle; and in that state it can learn enormously. Learning is then not merely the process of gathering information, but a discovery of the extraordinary riches that lie beyond the hope of the mind; and for the mind that makes this discovery, there is joy.

Watch yourself and you will see how you struggle from morning till night, and how your energy is wasted in this struggle. If you merely explain why you struggle, you get lost in explanations and the struggle continues; whereas, if you observe your mind very quietly without giving explanations, if you just let the mind be aware of its own struggle, you will soon find that there comes a state in which there is no struggle at all, but an astonishing watchfulness. In that state of watchfulness there is no sense of the superior and the inferior, there is no big man or little man, there is no guru. All those absurdities are gone because the mind is fully awake; and the mind that is fully awake is joyous.[27]

Discontent is the striving after 'the more', and contentment is the cessation of that struggle; but you cannot come to contentment without understanding the whole process of 'the more', and why the mind demands it.

We are struggling after something, and we have never paused to inquire if the thing we are after is worth struggling for. We have never asked ourselves if it's worth the effort, so we haven't yet discovered that it's not and withstood the opinion of our parents, of society, of all the Masters and gurus. It is only when we have understood the whole significance of 'the more' that we cease to think in terms of failure and success.

You see, we are so afraid to fail, to make mistakes. To make a mistake is considered terrible because we will be criticized for it, somebody will scold us. But, after all, why should you not make a mistake? Are not all the people in the world making mistakes? And would the world cease to be in this horrible mess if you were never to make a mistake?

Imitation is a form of stealing: you are nothing but he is somebody, so you are going to get some of his glory by copying him. This corruption runs right through human life, and very few are free of it. So what is important is to find out whether the inward emptiness can ever be filled. As long as the mind is seeking to fill itself it will always be empty. When the mind is no longer concerned with filling its own emptiness, then only does that emptiness cease to be.28

THE MIND IS EVERLASTINGLY ASKING for more and more, and our whole civilization is based upon the acquiring of the more, the demand for more properties, more money, more, more, and more; therefore there is always comparison, therefore everlastingly struggle.

Knowing envy, we say we must cultivate non-envy, which is another form of the more, negatively. So is it possible for the mind not to think in terms of the more at all, not to compare, not to judge what it is. This is not stagnation; on the contrary, when the mind is not seeking the more, when it is not comparing, you are no longer concerned with time.

Time implies 'the more': "I will be something tomorrow," "I will be happy in the future," "I will be a rich man," "I will fulfill," "I will be loved," "I shall love," and so on. The comparative mind, the mind that is asking for the more, is the mind of time, of tomorrow, is it not? So, when such a mind says, "I must not be envious," it is again another form of time, is it not? Another form of comparison is, "I have been this, I shall be less than that." So, can the mind which is

66

seeking the more, stop completely from the demand of the more, which is envy? Do you understand the problem, sirs?

The problem is not how to be free from envy—which is a very small affair—but how not to think in terms of the more, how not to think comparatively, how not to think in terms of time, how not to think "I will be." Can the mind ever not think in terms of the more? Do not say it is not possible. You do not know. All that you do know is the more—more knowledge, more influence, more clothes, more property, more love. If you cannot get the more, then you want the less and less and less.

Now, is it possible for the mind not to think at all in those terms? First put the question. Do not help me to be free of envy. Can the mind cease to think in terms of the more? Put that question and listen—not only now, but when you go home, when you are taking the tramcar, sitting in the bus, when you are walking alone, when you see a sari. When you see a man going in a big car, the big politician, the big businessman, put that question and find out and listen to it. Then you will find the truth of the matter; then you will find that the truth frees the mind from the more.

The mind then is not the conscious mind making an effort to denude itself of the more. When the mind makes a conscious effort of not asking for more, it is another form of negation of the same thing, of the more; so in that, there is no answer. But if you put that question, you can only listen to it when you are not judging, when you don't want a result, when you don't want to use it to produce a certain action. It is only when you are listening, that it is possible for truth to come into being, which will free the mind from the more.[29]

WE WERE WALKING IN THE OPEN GARDENS near a huge hotel. There was a golden blue in the western sky and the noise of the buses, cars went by. There were young plants full of promise, watered daily. They were still building, creating the gardens and a bird was hovering in the sky, fluttering its wings rapidly before it plunged to the earth; and in the east, there was the nearing of the full moon. What was beautiful was none of these things but the vast emptiness that seemed to hold the earth. What was beautiful was the poor man with his head down, carrying a small bottle of oil.

Krishnamurti: What does sorrow mean in this country? How do the people in this country meet sorrow? Do they escape from sorrow through the explanation of karma? How does the mind in India operate when it meets sorrow? The Buddhist meets it in one way, the Christian in another way. How does the Hindu mind meet it? Does it resist sorrow, or escape from it? Or does the Hindu mind rationalize it?

Pupul Jayakar: Are there really many ways of meeting sorrow? Sorrow is pain—the pain of someone dying, the pain of separation. Is it possible to meet this pain in various ways?

K: There are various ways of escape but there is only one way of meeting sorrow. The escapes with which we are all familiar are really the ways of avoiding the greatness of sorrow. You see, we use explanations to meet sorrow but these explanations do not answer the question. The only way to meet sorrow is to be without any resistance, to be without any movement away from sorrow, outwardly or inwardly, to remain totally with sorrow, without wanting to go beyond it.

PJ: What is the nature of sorrow?

K: There is personal sorrow, the sorrow that comes with the loss of someone you love, the loneliness, the separation, the anxiety for the other. With death there is also the feeling that the other has ceased to be, and there was so much that he wanted to do. All this is personal sorrow. Then there is that man, ill-clad, dirty, with his head down; he is ignorant, ignorant not merely of book knowledge, but deeply, really ignorant. The feeling that one has for the man is not self-pity, nor is there an identification with that man; it is not that you are placed in a better position than he is and so you feel pity for him, but there is within one the sense of the timeless weight of sorrow in man. This sorrow has nothing personal about it. It exists.

PJ: While you have been speaking, the movement of sorrow has been operating within me. There is no immediate cause for this sorrow but it seems like a shadow, always with man. He lives, he loves, he forms attachments, and everything ends. Whatever the truth of what you say, in this there is such an infinitude of sorrow. How is it to end? There appears to be no answer. The other day you said that in sorrow is the whole movement of passion. What does it mean?

K: Is there a relationship between sorrow and passion? I wonder what sorrow is. Is there such a thing as sorrow without cause? We know the sorrow which is cause and effect. My son dies—in that is involved my identification with my son, my wanting him to be something which I am not, my seeking continuity through him; and when he dies all that is denied, and I find myself completely emptied of all hope. In that there is self-pity, fear; in that there is pain, which is the cause of sorrow. This is the lot of everyone. This is what we mean by sorrow.

Then also there is the sorrow of time, the sorrow of ignorance, not the ignorance of knowledge, but the ignorance of one's own destructive conditioning; the sorrow of not knowing oneself; the sorrow of not knowing the beauty that lies at the depth of one's being and the going beyond. Do we see that when we escape from sorrow through various forms of explanation, we are really frittering away an extraordinary happening?

PJ: Then what does one do?

K: You have not answered my question, "Is there a sorrow without cause and effect?" We know sorrow and the

69

movement away from sorrow. Man has lived with sorrow from immemorial times. He has never known how to deal with it. So he has either worshiped it or run away from it. They are both the same movement. My mind does not do either, nor does it use sorrow as a means of awakening. Then what takes place?

PJ: All other things are the products of our senses. Sorrow is more than that. It is a movement of the heart.

K: I am asking you what is the relationship between sorrow and love.

PJ: Both are movements of the heart; the one is identified as joy and the other as pain.

K: Is love pleasure? Would you say joy and pleasure are the same? Without understanding the nature of pleasure, there is no depth to joy. You cannot invite joy. Joy happens. The happening can be turned into pleasure. When that pleasure is denied, there is the beginning of sorrow. Pleasure I can invite, pleasure I can pursue. If pleasure is love, then love can be cultivated.

PJ: We know pleasure is not love. Pleasure may be one manifestation of love, but it is not love. Both sorrow and love emerge from the same source.

K: I asked what is the relationship between sorrow and love? Can there be love if there is sorrow—sorrow being all the things that we have talked about? In sorrow, there is a factor of separation, of fragmentation. Is there not a great deal of self-pity in sorrow? What is the relationship of all this to love? Has love dependency? Has love the quality of the 'me' and the 'you'?

When there is no movement of escape from sorrow, then love is. Passion is the flame of sorrow, and that flame can only be awakened when there is no escape, no resistance.

Which means what?—which means, sorrow has in it no quality of division.

What is relationship for a mind which has understood sorrow and therefore the ending of sorrow? What is the quality of the mind that is no longer afraid of ending, which is death? When energy is not dissipated through escape, then that energy becomes the flame of passion. Compassion means passion for all. Compassion is passion for all.[30]

PRIDE /
AMBITION

*H*AVE YOU EVER CONSIDERED what it is to be successful as a writer, as a poet, as a painter, as a businessman or politician? To feel that you have inwardly achieved a certain control over yourself which others do not have, or that you succeeded where others have failed; to feel that you are better than somebody else, that you have become a successful man, that you are respected, looked up to by others as an example— what does all this indicate?

Naturally, when you have this feeling, there is pride: I have done something, I am important. The feeling of 'I' is in its very nature a sense of pride. So pride grows with success; one is proud of being very important compared with other people. This comparison of yourself with another exists also in your pursuit of the example, the ideal, and it gives you hope, it gives you strength, purpose, drive, which only strengthens the 'I', the pleasurable feeling that you are much more important than anybody else; and that feeling, that sense of pleasure, is the beginning of pride.

Pride brings a great deal of vanity, an egotistic inflation. You can observe this in the older people and in yourself. When you pass an examination and feel that you are a little cleverer than another, a sense of pleasure comes in. It is the same when you outdo somebody in an argument, or when you feel that you are physically much stronger or more beautiful—immediately there is a sense of your own importance. This feeling of the importance of the 'me' inevitably brings conflict, struggle, pain because you have to maintain your importance all the time.

Suppose I am proud because I have achieved something. I have become the principal; I have been to England or to America; I have done great things, my photograph has appeared in the newspapers, and so on and so on. Feeling very proud, I say to myself, "How am I to be free of pride?"

Now, why do I want to be free of pride? That is the important question, not how to be free. What is the motive, what is the reason, what is the incentive? Do I want to be free of pride because I find it harmful to me, painful, spiritually not good? If that is the motive, then to try to free myself from pride is another form of pride, is it not? I am still concerned with achievement. Finding that pride is very painful, spiritually ugly, I say that I must be free of it. The 'I must be free' contains the same motive as the 'I must be successful'. The 'I' is still important, it is the center of my struggle to be free.

So, what matters is not how to be free of pride but to understand the 'I', and the 'I' is very subtle. It wants one thing this year and another thing next year; and when that turns out to be painful, it then wants something else. So, as long as the center of the 'I' exists, whether one is proud or so-called humble is of very little significance. They are only different coats to put on. When a particular coat appeals to me I put it on; and next year, according to my fancies, my desires, I put on another coat.

What you have to understand is how this 'I' comes into being. The 'I' comes into being through the sense of achievement in various forms. This does not mean that you must not act; but the feeling that you are acting, that you are achieving, that you must be without pride, has to be understood. You have to understand the structure of the 'I'. You have to be aware of your own thinking; you have to observe how you treat your mother and father, your teacher and the servant; you have to be conscious of how you regard those who are above you and those who are below you, those whom you respect and those whom you despise. All this reveals the ways of the 'I'. Through understanding the ways of the 'I,' there is freedom from the 'I'. That is what matters, not just how to be free of pride.[31]

WE HAVE HEARD PEOPLE SAY THAT, without ambition, we cannot do anything. In our schools, in our social life, in our relationship with each other, in anything we do in life, we feel that ambition is necessary to achieve a certain end, either personal or collective or social, or for the nation. You know what that word ambition means? To achieve an end, to have the drive, the personal drive, the feeling that without struggling, without competing, without pushing you cannot get anything done in this world.

Please watch yourself and those about you, and you will see how ambitious people are. A clerk wants to become the manager, the manager wants to become the boss, the minister wants to be the prime minister, the lieutenant wants to become the general. So each one has his ambition. We also encourage this feeling in schools. We encourage students to compete, to be better than somebody else.

All our so-called progress is based on ambition. If you draw, you must draw much better than anybody else; if you make an image, it must be better than that made by anybody else; there is this constant struggle. What happens in this process is that you become very cruel. Because you want to achieve an end, you become cruel, ruthless, thoughtless, in your group, in your class, in your nation.

Ambition is really a form of power, the desire for power over myself and over others, the power to do something better than anybody else. In ambition, there is a sense of comparison; and therefore, the ambitious man is never really a creative man, is never a happy man; in himself he is discontented. And yet, we think that without ambition we should be nothing, we should have no progress.

Is there a different way of doing things without ambition, a different way of living, acting, building, inventing, without this struggle of competition, in which there is cruelty and which ultimately ends in war? I think there is a different way. But that way requires doing something contrary to all the established customs of thought.

When we are seeking a result, the important thing is the result, not the thing we do, in itself. Can we understand and

74

love the thing which we are doing, without caring for what it will produce, what it will get us, or what name or what reputation we will have?

Success is an invention of a society which is greedy, which is acquisitive. Can we, each one of us, as we are growing, find out what we really love to do—whether it is mending a shoe, becoming a cobbler, or building a bridge, or being a capable and efficient administrator? Can we have the love of the thing in itself without caring for what it will give us, or what it will do in the world? If we can understand that spirit, that feeling, then, I think, action will not create misery as it does at the present time; then we shall not be in conflict with one another.

But it is very difficult to find out what you really love to do, because you have so many contradictory urges. When you see an engine going very fast, you want to be an engine driver. When you are young, there is an extraordinary beauty in the engine. I do not know if you have watched it. But, later on, that stage passes and you want to become an orator, a speaker, a writer, or an engineer, and that too passes. Gradually, because of our rotten education, you are forced into a particular channel, into a particular groove. So you become a clerk or a lawyer or a mischief-monger; and in that job, you live, you compete; you are ambitious, you struggle.

Is it not the function of education, while you are very young, to help to bring about such intelligence in each one of you that you will have a job that is congenial to you and which you love and want to do; that you will not do a job which you hate or with which you are bored but which you have to do—because you are already married or because you have the responsibility of your parents, or because your parents say that you must be a lawyer when you really want to be a painter? Is it not very important, while you are young, for the teacher to understand this problem of ambition and to prevent it, by talking it over with each one of you, by explaining, by going into the whole problem of competition? This will help you to find out what you really want to do.

Now, we think in terms of doing something which will give us a personal benefit or a benefit to society or to the nation. We grow to maturity without maturing inwardly, without knowing what we want to do, but being forced to do something in which our heart is not. So, we live in misery. But society—that is, your parents, your guardians, your friends, and everybody about you—says what a marvelous person you are, because you are a success.

We are ambitious. Ambition is not only in the outer world but also in the inner world, in the world of the psyche and of the spirit. There also we want to be a success, we want to have the greatest ideals. This constant struggle to become something is very destructive; it disintegrates, it destroys. Can't you understand this urge to 'become', and concern yourself with being whatever you are, and then, from there, move on? If I am jealous, can I know I am jealous or envious, and not try to become nonenvious mentally? Jealousy is self-enclosing. If I know I am jealous and watch it, and let it be, then I will see that out of that, something extraordinary comes.

The becomer, whether in the outer world or in the spiritual world, is a machine, he will never know what real joy is. One will know joy only when one sees what one is and lets that complexity, that beauty, that ugliness, that corruption act without attempting to become something else. To do this is very difficult because the mind is always wanting to be something. You want to become philosophers, or become great writers. You worship the god of success, not the thing 'that is'. However poor you may be, however empty, however dull, if you can see the thing as it is, then that will begin to transform itself. But a mind occupied in becoming something never understands the being. The understanding of the being of what one is, that brings an extraordinary elation, a release of creative thought, creative life.

All the religious books, all our education, all our social, cultural approaches are to achieve, to become something. But that has not created a happy world; it has brought enormous misery. We live with ambition. That is our daily bread. But that bread poisons us, produces in us all kinds of misery, mentally and physically, so that the moment we are thwarted and prevented from carrying out our ambition, we fall ill. But a man who has the inward feeling of doing the thing which he loves, without thinking of an end, without thinking of a result—that man has no frustrations, he has no hindrances, he is the real creator.[32]

AMBITION AND INTEREST ARE TWO DIFFERENT THINGS, are they not? If I am really interested in painting, if I love to paint, then I do not compete to be the best or the most famous painter. I just love painting. You may be better at painting than I, but I do not compare myself with you. When I paint, I love what I am doing, and for me that is sufficient in itself.[33]

IF THE MIND IS IN A STATE OF COMPARISON, it creates problems and is everlastingly caught in them, and therefore it is never free. From childhood we have been brought up to compare: the Greek architecture, the Egyptian, the modern; to compare with the leader, the better, the more cultured, the more cunning; to be the perfect example, to follow the master; to compare, compare, compare, and therefore to compete. Where there is comparison, there must be conflict and contradiction, obviously—which means ambition. Those three are linked together inevitably. Comparison comes with competition, and competition is essentially ambition.

And yet you know every society is based on this competition. The more, the more, the more, the better—the world is caught up in it and every individual is in it. We say that if we have no ambition, if we have no goal, if we have no aim, we are just decaying. This is so deeply rooted in our minds, in our hearts—this thing to achieve, to arrive, to be.

Now, is it possible to see the process of this conflict? The very perception of this conflict, perceiving, seeing the very source of this conflict—not what you should do about it—has its own action. Now do we see that? That is all I am asking.

What is the good of saying, "It is inevitable. What will happen if I don't compete in the society which is competitive, which is ambitious, which is authoritative? What will happen to me?" That is not the problem. You will answer it later. But can we see the fact that a mind which is in conflict is the most destructive mind and whatever it wants to do, any activity, however reformative, has in it the seed of destruction.

Do I see it as I see a cobra, that it is poisonous? That is the crux of the whole matter. And if I see it, I do not have to do a thing about it, it has its own action. Why discuss everything else: how to build character, what should you do and what should you not do, and how can we find it? Surely, to uncover the source of love, the mind must be extraordinarily free from conflict. So, can the mind be free from conflict, which means competition and all the rest of it?[34]

PERHAPS IF WE CAN GO into the question of initiative then there may be a possibility of understanding self-fulfillment. For most of us fulfillment in some form or other becomes urgent, becomes necessary. In the process of fulfilling, so many problems, so many contradictions, so many conflicts arise; and there is everlasting misery in fulfillment. And yet, we do not know how to escape from it, how to act without fulfilling; for in the very fulfillment of action there is sorrow.

Action is not merely doing something, but is it not also thinking? Most of us are concerned with doing something; and if that action is satisfactory, if it sufficiently guarantees the fulfillment of one's desires, cravings, longings, then we are easily pacified. But if we do not discover the incentive that lies behind the urge to fulfill, surely we shall always be haunted by fear, with frustration; so is it not necessary to find out what this incentive is that is driving us? It may be clothed in different paints, with different intentions, with different meanings; but perhaps if we can hesitatingly, tentatively explore this question of incentive, then we shall begin to understand an action or a thought which is not always born from this consciousness of fulfillment.

Most of our incentives spring from ambitions, from pride, from the desire to be secure or to be well thought of. Now, you may say or I may say that my action is the outcome of the desire to do good, or to find the right values, or to have an ideology, a system that is incorruptible, or to do something that is essentially worthwhile, and so on. But behind all these words, all these pleasant-sounding phrases, is not the motive—the urge in some form or another—ambition? I want to achieve; I want to arrive; I want to have comfort, to know a certainty of mind in which there is no conflict.

My incentive is to achieve a result and to be assured of that result, in the same way as the man who accumulates money and who also seeks security; so in both these forces, there is the drive which we call ambition, upon which all our activities, our outlook, our energies, are spent. Is it possible to act without these ambitions, without these desires to fulfill? That is, I want to fulfill—I want to fulfill through my nation, through my children, through property, through name—I want to be 'somebody'. And the pride of being somebody is extraordinary, because it gives extraordinary energy without doing anything, merely the sense of being proud in itself is sufficient to keep me going, to keep me resisting, controlling, shaping.

You watch your own minds in operation. You will see the activities and you will see that behind them, however much you may cover them up with pleasant words, the drive is for fulfillment, for being somebody, to achieve a result. In this drive of ambition, there is competition, ruthlessness; and our whole structure of society is based on that.

The ambitious man is looked upon as being worthwhile, as being somebody who is good for society, who will through his ambition create a right environment and so on and so on. Or—we condemn ambition when it is worldly; we do not condemn it when we call it spiritual. A man who has given up the world, renounced it, and is seeking, he is not condemned. Is he not also driven by ambition to be something?

Everyone of us is seeking fulfillment—fulfillment through ideas, fulfillment through capacity, fulfillment through release in painting, through writing a poem, in loving, in being generous, in trying to be well-thought of. So, are not all our activities the outcome of this urge to fulfill? And behind that urge is ambition. When I hear that, when I know that, and when I realize that where there is fulfillment there must be sorrow, what am I to do? Do you follow what I mean?

I realize my life is based on ambition. Though I try to cover it up, though I suffer, though I sacrifice myself for an idea, all my activities are an outlet for self-fulfillment. You see me burnt out and you set yourself to do something worthwhile; that 'worthwhileness' is still the urge for fulfillment. This is our life, this is our constant urge, our constant pursuit, conscious as well as unconscious. When I realize this, when I know the content of all this struggle, what am I to do?

This urge to fulfill is one of our most fundamental problems, is it not? This urge to fulfill is in little things and in big things—to be somebody in my house, to dominate over my wife, my children, and to submit myself in the office, in order to rise, in order some day to be somebody. So, that is the process of my life, that is the process of all our lives. Then how is such a mind to put aside the desire for fulfillment? How am I to free myself from ambition?

I see that ambition is a form of self-fulfillment, and where there is fulfillment there is always the sense of being down and out, of being broken, frustrated; there is fear, a sense of utter loneliness, of despair and everlasting hope.

Is there any activity, any form of movement of the mind, which is not based on this? If I brush aside, control, shape ambition, it is still ambition, because I say, "It does not pay me to do this; but if I do that, that will pay me." If I say I must not fulfill, then there is the conflict of not fulfilling, the resistance against the desire; and the very resistance against the desire to fulfill becomes another form of fulfillment.

Why is the mind seeking fulfillment? Why is the mind, the 'me', which is the thought, why is it proud, ambitious? Why does it want to be well-thought-of? Can I understand that? Can the mind realize what it is that is pushing outwardly all the time? And when the outward movement of consciousness is cut, then it turns inward, and there again it is thwarted.

So our consciousness is this constant breathing in and out—to be important and not to be; to receive and to reject—this is our daily life of consciousness. And behind it, the mind is seeking a way out. If I can understand that, can know its full significance, then perhaps it is possible to have action which is not of ambition, which is not of pride, which is not of fulfillment, which is not of the mind.

To seek God, to try to find God, is another form of pride; and is it possible for me and you to find out what it is that is making us continuously go out and come in, go out and come in? Are we not aware of a state of emptiness in us, a state of despair, of loneliness, the complete sense of not being able to depend on anything, not having anybody to look up to? Don't we know a moment of extraordinary loneliness, of extraordinary sorrow, without reason, a sense of despair at the height of success, at the height of pride, at the height of thought, at the height of love; don't we know this loneliness? And is this loneliness not pushing us always to be somebody, to be well-thought-of?

Can I live with that loneliness, not run away from it, not try to fulfill through some action, and not try to transform it, not try to shape and control it? If the mind can, then perhaps it will go beyond that loneliness, beyond that despair; which does not mean into hope, into a state of devotion. Can I understand and live in that loneliness, not run away from it but live in that strange loneliness which comes when I am bored, when I am afraid, when I am apprehensive, not for any cause, or with cause? When I know this sense of loneliness, is it possible for the mind to live with it without trying to push it away?

Please listen to this; do not just listen to the mere words. As I talk, if you have observed your own minds, you will have come to that state of loneliness. It is with you now. This is not hypnosis because I suggest it; but actually if you have followed

the workings of your own mind, you will have come to that
state of loneliness; to be stripped of everything, every pre-
tense, every pride, every virtue, every action. Can the mind
live with that? Can the mind stay with it without any form of
condemnation? Can it look at it without interfering—not as
the observer looking at it? Is not then the mind itself that
state? Do you follow?

If I look at loneliness, then the mind operates on the
loneliness, tries to shape it or control it or run away from it.
The mind itself, not as the observer, is alone, lonely, empty.
It cannot tolerate for a single minute a state in which it is
completely empty, a state in which it does not know, a state
in which there is no action of knowing. So a mind seeing that
is fearful of it, it runs away into some activity of fulfillment.

Now, if the mind can stay in that very extraordinary sense
of being cut off from everything, from all ideas, from all
crutches, from all dependences, then is it not possible, for
such a mind to go beyond, not theoretically but actually? It is
only when it can fully experience that state of loneliness, that
state of emptiness, that state of nondependency, that it is possible to bring about an action which is without ambition.
Then only is it possible to have a world in which there is no
competition, no ruthless pursuit of self-enclosing activity.
Then that action is not the action through the narrow funnel
of the 'me'. That action is not self-enclosing. You will find
that such an action is creative, because it is without motive,
without ambition, it is not seeking a result. But to find that,
must the mind go through all this? Can it not suddenly
jump?

The mind can jump if I know how to listen. If I am listening rightly now, without any barrier, without any interpretation, with an open door to discover, there is freedom; and
through freedom alone I can discover.

That freedom is the freedom from fear, the freedom from
being well-thought-of, the freedom from pride, the freedom
from the desire to fulfill. And that freedom cannot come
about except through the realization of the complete negation of all thought, when the mind is totally empty, lonely,

when the mind is in a state in which there is neither despair nor fulfillment. Then only is there a possibility of a world in which ruthlessness, brutality, competition can come to an end.[35]

THE PSYCHOLOGICAL STRUCTURE OF SOCIETY is what we are, what we think, what we feel—the envy, the ambition, the everlasting struggle of contradiction, both conscious and unconscious—and we are caught in that. To break through it, we think we must make a great deal of effort. But effort always implies conflict, contradiction, does it not? When there is no contradiction, there is no effort: you live. But there is contradiction brought about by the psychological structure of the society in which we live; there is a conflict, a battle going on within each one of us all the time, con-sciously or unconsciously; and I feel that until this whole psy-chological structure is completely understood and broken through, we cannot possibly live a full life or understand that which is beyond the mind.

You see, the world is becoming more and more superficial. There is increasing prosperity throughout the world. There is the welfare state, and great progress is being made in many directions; but inwardly we have remained more or less static, pursuing the same old patterns, the same beliefs. We may alter our dogmas occasionally to suit circumstances, but we are liv-ing our lives very superficially. We are always scratching on the surface and never going below. And however superficially clever we are, however much knowledge or information we may have about so many things, until we alter completely, deep down, the whole psychological structure of our being, I don't see how we can be free and so be creative.

So I would like to consider with you this evening how to bring about a revolution, a psychological revolution, without effort. I am using the word *effort* in the sense of striving, try-ing to achieve or become something; of a mind that is caught in contradiction, that is struggling to overcome, to discipline, to conform, to adjust, to bring about a change within itself— I am using the word *effort* to cover all that.

Now, is it possible to bring about a total revolution without effort, not only in the conscious mind but also deep down, in the unconscious? For when we make an effort to bring about a psychological revolution within ourselves, it implies pressure, influence, a motive, a direction, all of which is the result of our conditioning.

Our conditioning, conscious and unconscious, is very deep and heavy, is it not? We are Christians, Hindus, Englishmen, Frenchmen, Germans, Indians, Russians; we belong to this or that church with all its dogmas, to this or that race with its burden of history. Superficially our minds are educated. The conscious mind is educated according to the culture we live in, and from that, one can perhaps disentangle oneself fairly easily. It is not too difficult to put aside being an Englishman, an Indian, a Russian, or whatever one happens to be, or to leave a particular church or religion. But it is much more difficult to uncondition the unconscious, which plays a far greater part in our life than the conscious mind.

The training of the conscious mind is useful and necessary as a means of earning a livelihood, or to perform a certain function—which is what our education is mostly concerned about. We are trained to do certain things, to function more or less mechanically in a certain way. That is our superficial education. But inwardly, unconsciously, deep down, we are the result of many thousands of years of man's endeavor; we are the sum total of his struggles, his hopes, his despairs, his everlasting search for something beyond, and this piling up of experience is still going on within us. To be aware of that conditioning, and to be free of it, demands a great deal of attention.

But to go very deeply into oneself, one must obviously be free of ambition, of competition, of envy, greed. And that's a very difficult thing to do, because envy, greed, and ambition are the very substance of the psychological social structure of which we are a part. Living as we are in a world made up of acquisitiveness, ambition, competition—to be entirely free of these things and yet not be destroyed by the world is really the problem.

If one observes, one is aware of how rapidly knowledge and technology are advancing in the world. Man will soon be able to go to the moon. Computers are taking over, and we ourselves are becoming more and more like machines, more and more automatic. Many of us go to the office day after day and are thoroughly bored with what we are doing, so we seek to escape from that boredom. And religion is a marvelous escape; or we turn to various forms of sensation and to drugs in order to feel more, to see more. This is going on throughout the world.

We are in perpetual conflict, not only with ourselves but with others. All our relationships are based on conflict, on possession, on acquisitiveness, on force. And when the mind is caught in such conflict, in such despair and anxiety, I don't see how one can go very far. But one has to go far. One has to destroy the whole psychological structure of society within oneself—destroy it completely. That is really the crux of our existence. Because we do lead a most superficial life; and we try to penetrate deeply by reading, by acquiring knowledge, by gaining more and more information. But all knowledge, all information is always on the surface.

So the question really is: how is one to live in this world without bringing about conflict, outwardly and especially inwardly? Because the inward conflict dictates the outward conflict. Only a mind that is really free of conflict, at every level, because it has no psychological problems of any kind—only such a mind can find out if there is something beyond itself.

Essentially our problem is not how to make more money, or how to stop the hydrogen bomb, or whether to join the Common Market—such problems are not very deep. They will be shaped and controlled by economic factors, by historical events, and by the innumerable pressures of sovereign governments, of societies and religions. What matters is to be capable of abstracting oneself from all that—not by withdrawing, not by becoming a monk or a nun, but by actually understanding its whole significance. One has to find out for oneself if it is at all possible to be completely free from the psychological structure of society—which is to be free of ambition.

I say it is entirely possible; but it is not easy. It is a very difficult thing to be free of ambition. Ambition implies 'the more', 'the more' implies time; and time means arriving, achieving. To deny time is to be free of ambition. I am not talking of chronological time—that you can't deny, for then you will miss your bus. But the psychological time which we have created for ourselves in order to become something inwardly—that you can deny. Which means, really, to die to tomorrow without despair.

You know, there are clever people, intellectuals who have examined the outward processes of man. They have examined society with its endless wars, they have examined the churches with their beliefs, dogmas, saviors; and after doing so, they are in despair. Out of despair they have contrived a philosophy of accepting the immediate, of not thinking about tomorrow but living as completely as possible in the now. I don't mean that at all. That's very easy. Any materialistic, shallow person can do it, and he doesn't have to be very clever. And that's what most of us do, unfortunately. We live for today, and today is extended into many tomorrows. I don't mean that at all. I mean to deny ambition totally and immediately; to die psychologically to the social structure so that the mind is never caught in time, in ambition, in the desire to be or not to be something.

You know, death is a marvelous thing; and to understand death requires a great deal of insight; to die to ambition naturally, without effort; to deny envy. Envy implies comparison, success, the pursuit of 'the more', you have more and I have less, you have a great deal of knowledge and I am ignorant. Can one end this process totally, instantly? One can end it, one can die totally to envy, ambition, competition, only when one is capable of looking at it without any distortion. There is distortion as long as there is motive. When you want to die to ambition in order to be something else, you are still ambitious. That's not dying at all. When you renounce with a motive, it is not renunciation. And inmost renunciations have behind them this motive to be, to achieve, to arrive, to find.

So it seems to me that we are merely becoming more and more clever, better and better informed. We are brought up on words, ideas, theories, knowledge, and there is very little empty space in the mind from which something can be seen clearly. It is only the empty mind that can see clearly, not the mind that's crammed with a lot of information and knowledge, nor the mind that's incessantly active, seeking, achieving, demanding. But a mind that's empty is not just blank. To be aware of an empty mind is extraordinarily difficult. And only in that emptiness is there understanding; only in that emptiness is there creation.

To come to that state of emptiness, one has to deny the whole social structure—the psychological structure of ambition, prestige, power. It is comparatively easy for older people not to be ambitious, to deny power and position; but such denials are very superficial. That's why it is so important to understand the unconscious. To understand the unconscious, that which is hidden and which you don't know, you cannot examine it with a positive, educated, analyzing mind. If you examine the unconscious by the conscious process of analysis, you are bound to create conflict.

Do please understand this, it is not very complicated. Our approach to any deep psychological problem is always a positive one. That is, we want to get at it, we want to control or resolve the problem, so we analyze it, or we pursue a particular system in order to understand it. But you can't understand something which you don't know by means of what you already know; you can't dictate what it should or should not be. You must approach it with empty hands; and to have empty hands, or an empty mind, is one of the most difficult things to do. Our minds are so full of the things that we have known; we are burdened with our memories, and every thought is a response of those memories. With positive thought we approach that which is not positive, the hidden, the unconscious.

Now, if, without any idea, without expecting to be told how, you can simply listen to what is being said, then I think you will find that you are able to approach the unconscious—which has such power, such an extraordinary drive, compulsion—without creating contradiction, and therefore without effort.

You don't have to accept my word for this, and I hope you won't, for then you would make me your authority, which would be a most ugly thing to do.

There is the unknowable, something far beyond the mind, beyond all thought. But you cannot possibly approach it with all your knowledge and memories, with the scars of experience, the weight of anxiety, guilt, fear. And you cannot get rid of these things by any effort whatsoever. You can be free of them only by listening to every thought and every feeling without trying to interpret what you hear; just listen, just observe and be attentive out of emptiness. Then you can live in this world untouched by its hatred, its ugliness, its brutality. You can function as a clerk, as a bus driver, as a bank manager, or what you will, without being caught in status. But the moment you bring to that function the psychological factors of ambition, authority, power, prestige, you cannot live in this world without everlasting sorrow.

Most of us really know all this. One doesn't need at all to listen to a talk of this kind. We know well enough that this is a terrible, brutal, ugly world, where every religion, every political faction is trying to shape man's thought; where the welfare state is making us more and more comfortable, dull, stupid, because we have used conflict as a means of becoming outwardly clever, bright. But inwardly we have not changed at all; we are carrying on as we have been for centuries: fearful, anxious, guilty, seeking power, seeking sex. We are perpetuating what is animalistic, which means that we are still functioning within the psychological structure of society.

The question is how to break that structure totally, how to destroy it completely and be out of it, without going insane and without becoming a monk, a nun, or a hermit. That structure can only be broken immediately, there is no time in which to do it. Either you do it immediately or never.[36]

ANGER

*E*VEN AT THAT ALTITUDE the heat was penetrating. The windowpanes felt warm to the touch. The steady hum of the plane's motor was soothing, and many of the passengers were dozing. The earth was far below us, shimmering in the heat, an unending brown with an occasional patch of green. Presently we landed, and the heat became all but unbearable; it was literally painful, and even in the shade of a building the top of one's head felt as if it would burst. The summer was well along and the country was almost a desert.

We took off again and the plane climbed, seeking the cool winds. Two new passengers sat in the opposite seats and they were talking loudly; it was impossible not to overhear them. They began quietly enough, but soon anger crept into their voices, the anger of familiarity and resentment. In their violence they seemed to have forgotten the rest of the passengers; they were so upset with each other that they alone existed, and no one else.

Anger has that peculiar quality of isolation; like sorrow, it cuts one off, and for the time being, at least, all relationship comes to an end. Anger has the temporary strength and vitality of the isolated. There is a strange despair in anger, for isolation is despair. The anger of disappointment, of jealousy, of the urge to wound gives a violent release whose pleasure is self-justification. We condemn others, and that very condemnation is a justification of ourselves. Without some kind of attitude, whether of self-righteousness or self-abasement, what are we? We use every means to bolster ourselves up; and anger, like hate, is one of the easiest ways.

Simple anger, a sudden flare-up which is quickly forgotten, is one thing; but the anger that is deliberately built up, that has been brewed and that seeks to hurt and destroy, is

quite another matter. Simple anger may have some physio-
logical cause which can be seen and remedied; but the anger
that is the outcome of a psychological cause is much more
subtle and difficult to deal with. Most of us do not mind
being angry, we find an excuse for it. Why should we not be
angry when there is ill-treatment of another or of ourselves?
So we become righteously angry. We never just say we are
angry, and stop there; we go into elaborate explanations of its
cause. We never just say that we are jealous or bitter but justify or explain it. We ask how there can be love without jealousy or say that someone else's actions have made us bitter,
and so on.

It is the explanation, the verbalization, whether silent or
spoken, that sustains anger, that gives it scope and depth.
The explanation, silent or spoken, acts as a shield against the
discovery of ourselves as we are. We want to be praised or
flattered, we expect something; and when these things do not
take place, we are disappointed, we become bitter or jealous.
Then, violently or softly, we blame someone else; we say the
other is responsible for our bitterness.

You are of great significance because I depend upon you
for my happiness, for my position or prestige. Through you,
I fulfill, so you are important to me; I must guard you, I
must possess you. Through you, I escape from myself; and
when I am thrown back upon myself, being fearful of my
own state, I become angry. Anger takes many forms: disappointment, resentment, bitterness, jealousy, and so on.

The storing up of anger, which is resentment, requires the
antidote of forgiveness; but the storing up of anger is far
more significant than forgiveness. Forgiveness is unnecessary
when there is no accumulation of anger. Forgiveness is essential if there is resentment; but to be free from flattery and
from the sense of injury, without the hardness of indifference,
makes for mercy, charity.

Anger cannot be got rid of by the action of will, for will is
part of violence. Will is the outcome of desire, the craving to
lie; and desire in its very nature is aggressive, dominant. To
suppress anger by the exertion of will is to transfer anger to a

different level, giving it a different name; but it is still part of violence. To be free from violence, which is not the cultivation of nonviolence, there must be the understanding of desire. There is no spiritual substitute for desire; it cannot be suppressed or sublimated. There must be a silent and choiceless awareness of desire; and this passive awareness is the direct experiencing of desire without an experiencer giving it a name.[37]

WHEREVER THERE IS A DIVISION there must be conflict. That's a law. An eternal law. Where there is separation, a division, a breaking up into two parts there must be conflict. And that conflict exists because we have separated the observer from the observed—I am different from my anger, I am different from my envy, I am different from my sorrow. Therefore being different, there is conflict, that is—"I must get rid of sorrow"; "Tell me how to overcome sorrow"; "Tell me what to do with my fear." So there is conflict, conflict all the time. But you are sorrow. You are not different from sorrow, are you? You are not different from anger, are you? You are not different from your sexual desires, are you? You are not different from the loneliness you feel—you are lonely.

Now, before, when I separated, I acted upon my sorrow. You understand? If I am lonely, I then escape from loneliness, try to overcome it or analyze it and try to fill the loneliness with all kinds of amusements or religious activity. Before, I acted upon it; now I can't act upon it because I am that. So what happens when the observer is the observed? You understand? When the anger is me, then what takes place?

First, all conflict ceases. All conflict ceases when you realize you are that. I am brown—finished. It's a fact—light brown or dark brown or purple or whatever color it is. So you eliminate altogether this divisive process which brings conflict in yourself.

The fact is, I am anger, I am jealous, I am lonely. Why do we make that into an idea, make an abstraction of it? Is it easier to make an abstraction rather than to face the fact?

Because then I can play with the idea. I say, "Yes, this is a good idea," "This is a bad idea." But when there is no abstraction but the fact, then I have to deal with it.[38]

FEAR, PLEASURE, SORROW, THOUGHT, and violence are all interrelated. Most of us take pleasure in violence, in disliking somebody, hating a particular race or group of people, having antagonistic feelings towards others. But in a state of mind in which all violence has come to an end, there is a joy which is very different from the pleasure of violence, with its conflicts, hatreds, and fears.

Can we go to the very root of violence and be free from it? Otherwise we shall live everlastingly in battle with each other. If that is the way you want to live—and apparently most people do—then carry on; if you say, "Well, I'm sorry, violence can never end," then you and I have no means of communication; you have blocked yourself. But if you say there might be a different way of living, then we shall be able to communicate with each other.

So let us consider together, those of us who can communicate, whether it is at all possible totally to end every form of violence in ourselves and still live in this monstrously brutal world. I think it is possible. I don't want to have a breath of hate, jealousy, anxiety, or fear in me. I want to live completely at peace. Which doesn't mean that I want to die. I want to live on this marvelous earth, so full, so rich, so beautiful. I want to look at the trees, flowers, rivers, meadows, women, boys, and girls, and at the same time live completely at peace with myself and with the world. What can I do?

If we know how to look at violence, not only outwardly in society—the wars, the riots, the national antagonisms and class conflicts—but also in ourselves, then perhaps we shall be able to go beyond it.

Here is a very complex problem. For centuries upon centuries man has been violent; religions have tried to tame him throughout the world and none of them have succeeded. So if we are going into the question, we must—it seems to me— be at least very serious about it, because it will lead us into quite a different domain; but if we want merely to play with the problem for intellectual entertainment, we shall not get very far.

You may feel that you yourself are very serious about the problem, but that as long as so many other people in the world are not serious and are not prepared to do anything about it, what is the good of your doing anything. I don't care whether they take it seriously or not. I take it seriously, that is enough. I am not my brother's keeper. I myself, as a human being, feel very strongly about this question of violence, and I will see to it that in myself I am not violent. But I cannot tell you or anybody else, "Don't be violent." It has no meaning—unless you yourself want it. So if you yourself really want to understand this problem of violence, let us continue on our journey of exploration together.

Is this problem of violence out there or here? Do you want to solve the problem in the outside world, or are you questioning violence itself as it is in you? If you are free of violence in yourself, the question is, "How am I to live in a world full of violence, acquisitiveness, greed, envy, brutality? Will I not be destroyed?" That is the inevitable question which is invariably asked. When you ask such a question it seems to me you are not actually living peacefully. If you live peacefully you will have no problem at all. You may be imprisoned because you refuse to join the army or shot because you refuse to fight—but that is not a problem; you will be shot. It is extraordinarily important to understand this.

We are trying to understand violence as a fact, not as an idea, as a fact which exists in the human being, and the human being is myself. And to go into the problem, I must be completely vulnerable, open to it. I must expose myself to myself—not necessarily expose myself to you, because you may not be interested—but I must be in a state of mind that demands to see this thing right to the end and at no point stops and says: I will go no further.

Now it must be obvious to me that I am a violent human being. I have experienced violence in anger, violence in my

93

sexual demands, violence in hatred, creating enmity, violence in jealousy and so on—I have experienced it, I have known it, and I say to myself, "I want to understand this whole problem, not just one fragment of it expressed in war, but this aggression in man which also exists in the animals and of which I am a part."

Violence is not merely killing another. It is violence when we use a sharp word, when we make a gesture to brush away a person, when we obey because there is fear. So violence isn't merely organized butchery in the name of God, in the name of society or country. Violence is much more subtle, much deeper, and we are inquiring into the very depths of violence.

When you call yourself an Indian or a Muslim or a Christian or a European, or anything else, you are being violent. Do you see why it is violent? Because you are separating yourself from the rest of mankind. When you separate yourself by belief, by nationality, by tradition, it breeds violence. So a man who is seeking to understand violence does not belong to any country, to any religion, to any political party or partial system; he is concerned with the total understanding of mankind.

There are two primary schools of thought with regard to violence—one which says, "Violence is innate in man" and the other which says, "Violence is the result of the social and cultural heritage in which man lives." We are not concerned with which school we belong to—it is of no importance. What is important is the fact that we are violent, not the reason for it.

One of the most common expressions of violence is anger. When my wife or sister is attacked, I say I am righteously angry; when my country is attacked, my ideas, my principles, my way of life, I am righteously angry. I am also angry when my habits are attacked or my petty little opinions. When you tread on my toes or insult me I get angry, or if you run away with my wife and I get jealous, that jealousy is called righteous because she is my property. And all this anger is morally justified. But to kill for my country is also justified.

So when we are talking about anger, which is a part of violence, do we look at anger in terms of righteous and unrighteous anger according to our own inclinations and environmental drive, or do we see only anger? Is there righteous anger ever? Or is there only anger? There is no good influence or bad influence, only influence, but when you are influenced by something which doesn't suit me, I call it an evil influence.

The moment you protect your family, your country, a bit of colored rag called a flag, a belief, an idea, a dogma, the thing that you demand or that you hold—that very protection indicates anger. So can you look at anger without any explanation or justification, without saying, "I must protect my goods," or "I was right to be angry," or "How stupid of me to be angry"? Can you look at anger as if it were something by itself? Can you look at it completely objectively, which means neither defending it nor condemning it? Can you?

Can I look at you if I am antagonistic to you, or if I am thinking what a marvelous person you are? I can see you only when I look at you with a certain care in which neither of these things is involved. Now, can I look at anger in the same way, which means that I am vulnerable to the problem, I do not resist it, I am watching this extraordinary phenomenon without any reaction to it?

It is very difficult to look at anger dispassionately because it is a part of me, but that is what I am trying to do. Here I am, a violent human being, whether I am black, brown, white, or purple. I am not concerned with whether I have inherited this violence, or whether society has produced it in me; all I am concerned with is whether it is at all possible to be free from it. To be free from violence means everything to me. It is more important to me than sex, food, position, for this thing is corrupting me. It is destroying me and destroying the world, and I want to understand it, I want to be beyond it. I feel responsible for all this anger and violence in the world. I feel responsible—it isn't just a lot of words—and I say to myself, "I can do something only if I am beyond

anger myself, beyond violence, beyond nationality."
This feeling I have that I must understand the violence in
myself brings tremendous vitality and passion to find
out.

To investigate the fact of your own anger, you must pass
no judgment on it, for the moment you conceive of its opposite, you condemn it and therefore you cannot see it as it is.
When you say you dislike or hate someone, that is a fact,
although it sounds terrible. If you look at it, go into it completely, it ceases, but if you say, "I must not hate; I must have
love in my heart," then you are living in a hypocritical world
with double standards. To live completely, fully, in the
moment is to live with *what is*, the actual, without any sense
of condemnation or justification—then you understand it so
totally that you are finished with it. When you see clearly, the
problem is solved.[39]

WHAT IS ANALYSIS? Analysis is observation, isn't it?—a form
of observation. I watch, and watching myself I say: I have
been angry, why have I been angry?—the explanations, the
cause, the justifications, all that is part of analysis, which is
part of thought, isn't it?

And analysis takes time. At the end of it I say: that anger
was justified or that anger was not justified, therefore I must
be watchful next time, I will only get angry when it is justified—righteous anger and unrighteous anger!

So look what is happening. Thought is awakened to anger
and watching anger. Then what takes place? The thought is
the observer, isn't it? Then the observer is different from the
thing which it observes, his anger. In observing thought and
all the activities of thought—out of that observation comes
intelligence. This intelligence is the result of observation of
the workings of thought.

Now, that intelligence is watching—watching the mind,
watching the body, watching the heart. That intelligence says:
don't eat that food—listen to this—because yesterday you
had pain, give it up. And because intelligence is in operation,
you give it up instantly.

Questioner: That's memory sir.

Krishnamurti: No, wait, listen carefully. I said, sir, intelligence is not thought. Intelligence comes into being in observing the operation of thought—observing, not condemning it or accepting it, just watching thought, how thought operates. In that watching intelligence comes. Now that intelligence is watching. And I eat the wrong things, when that intelligence is watching—listen to it—it's also aware of the causation which is the past. So intelligence doesn't neglect the cause; it is aware of the cause and the result. But it is not memory; it is intelligence which perceives the whole movement of causation.[40]

Look—I AM ANGRY, that's the only factor, isn't it? When I say: I must not be angry—that's a conclusion, that's an abstraction. But the fact is, I'm angry. If I know how to resolve that anger, its opposite wouldn't arise. Can I solve that anger without resorting to its opposite, saying "I must not be angry"? The 'I must not be angry' is its opposite. And that comes only when I can't understand the whole structure of anger and go beyond it.

So I say, can I understand anger, not control it, not reject it, not yield to it, but understand it, have an insight into the whole structure of anger? If I do, then the opposite doesn't exist.

Questioner: If I don't control my anger I'm afraid I'll kill someone.

Krishnamurti: Look, before you kill somebody, try to find out if you can resolve the anger. To control it is to suppress it. To say, "I must not be angry" is to create the opposite, and therefore a conflict between 'must not be' and the fact that I am. Or if you try to escape from it, anger is still there.

Look what has taken place. Before, I tried to control it, which is a wastage of energy. Before, I tried to suppress it, which is a wastage of energy. Before, I tried to escape from it or rationalize it, which is an avoidance, an escape from the fact. If I don't escape, control, suppress, or try to rationalize it, all that energy is concentrated, isn't it? So I have got that enormous energy to deal with one fact, which is anger. Have you got that? Please, otherwise we can't go on—if you haven't got it then it becomes merely verbal. You understand?

You're angry, your tradition, your culture says, "Suppress it, control it, escape from it, and rationalize it." I say, that is wasting your energy, which prevents you from observing the only factor, which is anger. So anger has no opposite, there is only that, and you have the energy.

Now, next step. Why do you call it anger? Because previously you have been angry, by naming it as anger, you have emphasized the previous experience. So you are observing the present factor with the previous experience, therefore conditioning the present factor. Are you meeting this? So the naming is a wastage of energy. So you do not name, no control, no suppression, no escape, and you have the energy. Then, is there anger?

Don't say you don't know, because you are then facing the only factor. And when you are facing completely that factor, the factor doesn't exist, because it exists only when you are escaping, fighting, controlling, suppressing. Right, you've got it?

There is in me—in one, in a human being—this duality. And I ask myself, "Is there a duality at all?" There is man, woman, sunshine, darkness—that's obvious, but psychologically, are there opposites? This requires attention, doesn't it? Because to see this clearly you need to observe.[41]

*F*REEDOM IS NOT A REACTION but rather the state of mind which comes into being when we understand reaction. Reaction is the response to challenge—it is pleasure, anger, fear, psychological pain—and in understanding this very complex structure of response, we shall come upon freedom. Then you will find that freedom is not freedom from anger, from authority, and so on. It is a state per se, to be experienced for itself, and not because you are against something.[42]

GUILT

WHAT IS GUILT? And what is its relationship to the ego, the whole consciousness of humankind, of man, of woman, and so on? What is guilt? Why does one have this enormous sense of guilt? It may be very, very superficial, or very, very deep-rooted from childhood, and allowed to grow as one gets older. And that feeling of guilt makes one feel very empty—you know all this—with a sense of not being able to do any-thing. And then out of that guilt, one builds a wall round himself. And that wall prevents any further communication. Or I am frightened of that guilt: you have told me to do something from childhood, and I can't do it, but I feel I must do it, and if I fail I feel guilty. And the parents play a terrible role in this. Sorry! They encourage this guilt, con-sciously or unconsciously, so that this guilt becomes part of the ego, part of me.

I think it would be wrong to put the question, what is the relationship between the two. You understand how the question is evolving? It is not two separate things. It is the outcome of feeling guilt, with other factors, that constitute the ego. They are not two separate activities or two separate reactions. So guilt is part of the psyche, part of the ego, part of the 'me'.

Now why does one feel guilt? People make you feel guilty and hold you in that state because it's very convenient for them; they like to bully you and bring about a sense of guilt, the feeling that you must submit, you must accept, you must obey. Though you revolt against it, you keep it underground and hold on to your guilt. And other factors make up the ego, the 'me'. Guilt makes one feel terribly lonely with a sense of depression, and if that guilt is very deep and strong, one can't resolve it. Therefore I come to you and say, "Please help me to overcome this guilt." And then you impose, if you are the boss, another reaction of guilt. So it goes on.

I am asking—we are asking, why does this feeling exist at all? It is encouraged, isn't it, in orthodox religions? In Christianity there is the original sin and the savior, and therefore I must feel guilty, and confession and the whole circus begins. Forgive me if I use that word. It takes different forms. In the Christian world confession, absolution. And in the Asiatic world it has a different form: they go to temples— you know, all kinds of things they do.

But is it necessary to feel that? Can there be an education in which there is nothing of this? I wonder. We are playing together, please. Is there a kind of bringing up a child in which there is not this encouragement of the feeling of guilt?

How to resolve guilt, how to get over it, becomes a problem. All kinds of things begin with it, and we make it into a problem. Now, what is a problem? Human beings apparently have thousands of problems: political, religious, economic, sexual, in relationship. Life, living becomes a problem, and part of it is generally associated with guilt.

Is it possible not to have a single problem—sexual, religious, political, economic, in relationship, and so on? So let's find out—you are playing the game with me—let's find out why human beings have problems.

From childhood, when a child goes to school, writing becomes a problem to him. Reading, spelling, then mathematics, geography, history, biology, chemistry, science, archaeology, and so on. So from the very beginning he is trained, or conditioned, to have problems. This is obvious. So his brain is conditioned to have problems. Are you playing the game with me? And all his life from the moment he is born practically until he dies, the brain continues to live in problems, because he has been educated, cultivated in the whole system of comparison, examinations, rewards, punishments, and so on. All that has made the brain not only receive problems but have its own problems; it's conditioned that way, therefore it can never solve any problem.

So is it possible to have a brain that has no problems but can answer problems? Because there are problems. Now, is that possible, because as long as you have problems you must have the feeling that you must resolve them and if you can't resolve them, you feel guilty. And so we keep this going. Then others come and help us, and the whole thing begins again in a different form.

Listen to the question. Go into the mechanism of guilt, its relation to the ego; and we said don't separate the two, because guilt is part of the ego, part of the 'me'. It's not separate. Therefore it's not something related to. It is in, it is there. Then we said, why do we have problems. Problems exist from childhood, from the child who goes to the school. He is educated to have problems. So his whole life becomes a problem: depression, anxiety, and so on. Then he goes and asks another; which means asking help from another. But the other is himself; the other has problems, gets depressed, feels lonely. So the other is you. I wonder if you realize this. Therefore what's the good of asking him?[43]

Questioner: I have done something wrong and sinful, and it has left me with a terrible feeling of guilt. How am I to get over this feeling?

Krishnamurti: Sir, what do you mean by sin? The Christians have a concept of sin which you have not, but you do feel guilty when you have more money, when you have a bigger house than somebody else—at least you should. [*Laughter*] When you are riding in a comfortable car and you see a queue of people one mile long waiting to catch a bus, it does something to you—either you have what is called a feeling of guilt, or you want to transform something radically, not in the stupid economic sense, but in the religious sense, so that these things cannot happen in the world. Or you may feel guilty because you realize that you have a certain capacity, an insight which others have not. But strangely we never feel guilty about such things, we feel guilty only about worldly things—having more money, a better social position, and so on.

Now, what is this sense of guilt, and when are you aware of it? Is it a form of pity? Most of us are occupied with ourselves in different ways from morning till night, and consciously or unconsciously we move along in that stream. When there is a sudden challenge, that movement of self-occupation is disturbed, and then we feel guilty, we feel that we are doing something wrong, or that we have not done something right; but that feeling is still within the stream of self-centered activity, is it not? I do not know if you are all following this.

Why should you feel guilty? If you are living intensely with your whole being, if you are fully aware of everything about you and within yourself, the unconscious as well as the conscious, where is there room for guilt? It is the man who lives in fragments, who is divided within himself, that feels guilty. One part of him is good, the other part corrupt; one part is trying to be noble, and the other is ignoble; one part is ambitious, ruthless, and the other part talks about peace, love. Such people feel guilty because they are still within the pattern of their own making. As long as there is self-centered activity, you cannot get over the feeling of guilt, it is impossible. That feeling disappears only when you approach life totally, with your whole being, that is, when there is no self-fulfillment of any kind. Then you will find that the sense of guilt does not exist at all because you are not thinking about yourself. There is no self-centered activity.

Sirs, if you are listening and are not acting, it is like a man who is always tilling and never sowing. It is better not to listen to a truth than to listen without acting, for then it becomes a poison. Whether you approve or disapprove of the details of what is said here is irrelevant; what matters is to see the truth that as long as you function within the field of self-centered activity, you are bound to have various kinds of sorrow and frustration. Sorrow and frustration cease only when you are living totally, with the intensity of your whole being, of your mind, heart, and body; and you cannot live with that completeness, with that intensity, if you are concerned about your own virtue. You may be free from the feeling of guilt

102

today, but it will arise in another form tomorrow, or the day after tomorrow.

Just try this, sirs, try a little bit to live intensely every day, with all your mind, heart, and body, with all your capacity, feeling, energy. Desire is contradictory in itself; but if you love intensely with your body, mind, and heart, with everything that you have, then you will find there is no contradiction, there is no sin. It is desire, envy, ambition that creates contradiction, and the mind caught in contradiction can never find that which is real.[44]

I FEEL GUILT, WHY DO I NAME IT? I name it instantly. The naming of it is the recognition of it, therefore I have had that feeling before. And having had it before, I recognize it now. Through recognition I strengthen what has happened before. I have strengthened the memory of the previous guilt by saying, "I feel guilty." So see what has happened. Every form of recognition strengthens the past. And recognition takes place through naming. So by and through recognition I strengthen the past.

Why does the mind do this? Why does it always strengthen the past by saying, "I have been guilty, I am guilty, it is terrible to be guilty, how am I to get rid of this guilt?"—why does it do it? Does it do it because the mind needs to be occupied with something? It needs to be occupied, whether with God, with smoke, with sex, with something, it has to be occupied, therefore it is afraid not to be occupied. And in occupation with the feeling of guilt, in that feeling there is a certain security. At least I have that thing; I have nothing else, but at least I have that feeling of being guilty.

So what is happening? Through recognition, which is the naming, the mind is strengthening a past feeling, which has happened before, and so the mind is constantly occupied with that feeling of guilt. That gives it a certain occupation, a certain sense of security, a certain action from that which becomes neurotic. So what takes place? Can I, when the feeling arises, observe it without naming?

So I find when I do not name, the thing no longer exists. And I am afraid—listen to this carefully—the mind is afraid of living in a state of nothingness. Therefore it has to have a word. The word has become tremendously important—my country, my god, my Jesus, my Krishna—the word. So the word—listen to this—the word is the past, the word is the memory, the word is the thought. So thought divides.

Look, I must have memory in order to go to my house. I must have memory to talk English. I must have memory to come here and sit on this platform. I must have memory for the language that I use. I have memory of riding a bicycle, or driving a car. So memory is absolutely essential, otherwise I couldn't function. Memory is knowledge, we must have knowledge. And that knowledge—listen to what takes place—that knowledge is words.

Now I have had the knowledge of previous guilt. When I call the present feeling guilt, I have strengthened the previous knowledge. And that knowledge is the observer. So the observer looks at that feeling which I have now and calls it guilt. And therefore in calling it guilt, the knowledge of the past is strengthened. It is fairly simple and clear.

Questioner: Who is the observer? Is the observer different from the many fragments?

Krishnamurti: He is one of the fragments, isn't he?

Q: But the feeling of myself is there.

K: I know it is there. That is the illusion. Wait sir. That is our culture, that is our verbal statement, that is the way we live. We say, "I have identified myself with my country, with my god, with my flag, my politics," and so on. I have been identifying with all those and I say, "How stupid of me, that has led to a lot of mischief, now I want to identify with myself." You see, I have discarded all the identifications outside of me, now I want to identify myself with myself.

What is myself? It is obviously a lot of images and words. And so I say, "Look at what I am doing. I am always trying to establish a fact, which becomes a nonfact, always trying to defend myself with an idea, with an image, with a conclusion, and those are all words." The mind is afraid of being completely empty, therefore it says, "I must be." It is so afraid of being empty, therefore it must be occupied with the kitchen, with sex, with God, with politics, with a dozen things, because it is so afraid to be completely empty.

The observer is the past, and the observed is the present. Now can the mind observe without naming the feeling which is the present?[45]

DESIRE

WHY ARE WE TORTURED BY DESIRE? Why have we made desire into a torturous thing? There is desire for power, desire for position, desire for fame, sexual desire, the desire to have money, to have a car, and so on. What do you mean by that word *desire*? And why is it wrong? Why do we say we must suppress or sublimate desire, do something about it? We are trying to find out. Don't just listen to me, but go into it with me and find out for yourself.

What is wrong with desire? You have suppressed it, have you not? Most of you have suppressed desire, for various reasons—because it is not convenient, not satisfactory, or because you think it is not moral, or because the religious books say that to find God you must be without desire, and so on. Tradition says you must suppress, control, dominate desire, so you spend your time and energy in disciplining yourself.

Now, let us first see what happens to a mind that is always controlling itself, suppressing, sublimating desire. Such a mind, being occupied with itself, becomes insensitive. Though it may talk about sensitivity, goodness, though it may say that we must be brotherly, we must produce a marvelous world, and all the rest of the nonsense that people talk who suppress desire—such a mind is insensitive because it does not understand that which it has suppressed.

Whether you suppress or yield to desire, it is essentially the same because the desire is still there. You may suppress the desire for a woman, for a car, for position; but the very urge not to have these things, which makes you suppress the desire for them, is itself a form of desire. So, being caught in desire, you have to understand it, and not say it is right or wrong.

106

Now, what is desire? When I see a tree swaying in the wind, it is a lovely thing to watch, and what is wrong with that? What is wrong in watching the beautiful motion of a bird on the wing? What is wrong in looking at a new car, marvelously built and highly polished? And what is wrong in seeing a nice person with a symmetrical face, a face that shows good sense, intelligence, quality?

But desire does not stop there. Your perception is not just perception, but with it comes sensation. With the arising of sensation, you want to touch, to contact, and then comes the urge to possess. You say, "This is beautiful, I must have it," and so begins the turmoil of desire.

Now, is it possible to see, to observe, to be aware of the beautiful and the ugly things of life, and not say, "I must have," or "I must not have"? Have you ever just observed anything? Do you understand, sirs? Have you ever observed your wife, your children, your friends, just looked at them? Have you ever looked at a flower without calling it a rose, without wanting to put it in your buttonhole, or take it home and give it to somebody? If you are capable of so observing, without all the values attributed by the mind, then you will find that desire is not such a monstrous thing.

You can look at a car, see the beauty of it, and not be caught in the turmoil or contradiction of desire. But that requires an immense intensity of observation, not just a casual glance. It is not that you have no desire, but simply that the mind is capable of looking without describing. It can look at the moon and not immediately say, "That is the moon—how beautiful it is," so there is no chattering of the mind coming in between. If you can do this, you will find that in the intensity of observation, of feeling, of real affection, love has its own action, which is not the contradictory action of desire.

Experiment with this and you will see how difficult it is for the mind to observe without chattering about what it observes. But surely, love is of that nature, is it not? How can you love if your mind is never silent, if you are always thinking about yourself? To love a person with your whole being, with your mind, heart, and body requires great intensity; and when love is intense, desire soon disappears. But most of us have never had this intensity about anything, except about our own profit, conscious or unconscious; we never feel for anything without seeking something else out of it. But only the mind that has this intense energy is capable of following the swift movement of truth.

Truth is not static, it is swifter than thought, and the mind cannot possibly conceive of it. To understand truth, there must be this immense energy, which cannot be conserved or cultivated. This energy does not come through self-denial, through suppression. On the contrary, it demands complete abandonment; and you cannot abandon yourself, or abandon everything that you have, if you merely want a result.[46]

WHAT IS DESIRE? Does desire bring about clarity? And therefore that clarity is skill in action? In the field of desire does compassion flower? You have to ask these questions. To find out the truth of the matter, you must examine what is desire, not desire for the object; the objects are not important, they vary—from childhood you desire a toy and so on, as you grow older you desire something else. We are not discussing, or talking over together the objects of desire but actually what is desire. If it does not bring clarity, and if desire is not the field in which beauty and the greatness of compassion flower, then what place has desire? You must go into it and find out—not according to any psychologist, any preacher, including the speaker—but go into it together to find out. We are insisting that we think together, reason together, find out together. Not I find, and then you accept or reject, but together find out.

So what is desire? The desire for a better society, and the cultivation of that desire becomes passion for an idea. People are so committed to communism, they are passionate about it or any other form of ideological projection. So it becomes very important to go into this question of what desire is— not how to suppress it, how to run away from it, how to make it more beautiful—but just what desire is. How does it come about that human beings are caught in this? One year you are a Christian, or for thirty years a Christian, then you throw that out and join some other label called Hindu, or Buddhist, or Zen, or whatever it is.

In inquiring we must deal with facts, not with opinions, not with judgments—then you have your opinions and the speaker may have his opinions and so there is a battle, therefore there is no communication. But we are going into facts—not your fact or my fact, but the fact that human beings have colossal desires, absurd desires, illusory desires. So what is desire? How does it come? Go into it. Look at it. You have your own desires, unfortunately, or fortunately. Desire to be good—how does that desire arise in you? You see a beautiful woman or a beautiful man—see. Perception, the seeing, then the contact, then the sensation, then that sensation is taken over by thought, which becomes desire with its image. Follow it yourself and you will see it.

You see a beautiful vase, a beautiful sculpture, a beautiful statue, the ancient Egyptian, or the Greek, and you look at it. As you look at it, if they allow you to touch it, you touch it. See the depth of that figure as he sits on a chair, or sits cross-legged. From that there is a sensation, isn't there?—"What a marvelous thing." And from that sensation the desire says, "I wish I had that in my room. I wish I could look at it every day, touch it every day." There comes the pride of possession to have such a marvelous thing like that. That is desire, isn't it? Seeing, contact, sensation; then thought using that sensation to cultivate the desire to possess, or not to possess. This is obvious. This is not my explanation. It is a factual explanation.

Now comes the difficulty: realizing that the religious people throughout the world have said, "Don't look. When a woman comes near you look at something else. Think of her as your sister, mother, God,"—or whatever it is! (Laughter.) You laugh but you are born in this. You are conditioned to this. So all the religious people have said, "Take vows of celibacy. Don't look at a woman. If you do look, treat her as your sister, mother, whatever you like, because you are in the service of God and you need all your energy to serve him. In the service of God you are going to have great tribulations, therefore be prepared, but don't waste your energy." But the thing is boiling, right? We are trying to understand that which is boiling. Not to look at a woman or a man, but that which is the desire, which is constantly boiling, which wants to fulfill, wants to complete itself.

We said desire is the movement of perception, seeing, contact, sensation, thought as desire with its image. Now we are saying that seeing, touching, sensation is normal, healthy—end it there. Don't let thought come and take it over and make it into a desire. Do understand this and then you will see that there will be no suppression of desire.

That is, you see a beautiful house, well proportioned, lovely windows, beautiful garden, well kept, with a roof that melts into the sky, walls that are thick and part of the earth. You look at it, there is sensation. You touch it—you may not actually touch it, but you touch it with your eyes—you smell the air, the herbs, the newly cut grass. And can't you end it there? Why does sensation become desire? When there is perception, contact, sensation, it is natural, it is beautiful to see the lovely things, or an ugly thing. Then to end it there say, "It is a beautiful house." Then there is no registration as thought which says, "I wish I had that house"—which is desire and the continuation of desire. You can do this so easily—and I mean easily—if you understand the nature of desire.[47]

Questioner: We know sex as an inescapable physical and psychological necessity, and it seems to be a root cause of chaos in the personal life of our generation. How can we deal with this problem?

Krishnamurti: Why is it that whatever we touch we turn into a problem? We have made God a problem, we have made love a problem, we have made relationship, living a problem, and we have made sex a problem. Why? Why is everything we do a problem, a horror? Why are we suffering? Why has sex become a problem?

Why do we submit to living with problems, why do we not put an end to them? Why do we not die to our problems instead of carrying them day after day, year after year? Sex is certainly a relevant question, but there is the primary question: why do we make life into a problem? Working, sex, earning money, thinking, feeling, experiencing—you know, the whole business of living—why is it a problem?

What do we mean by the problem of sex? Is it the act, or is it a thought about the act? Surely it is not the act. The sexual act is no problem to you any more than eating is a problem to you, but if you think about eating or anything else all day long because you have nothing else to think about, it becomes a problem to you. Is the sexual act the problem, or is it the thought about the act?

Why do you think about it? Why do you build it up?— which you are obviously doing. The cinemas, the magazines, the stories, the way women dress, everything is building up your thought of sex. Why does the mind build it up, why does the mind think about sex at all? Why? Why has it become a central issue in your life? When there are so many things calling, demanding your attention, you give complete attention to the thought of sex.

What happens, why are your minds so occupied with it? Because that is a way of ultimate escape, is it not? It is a way of complete self-forgetfulness. For the time being, at least for that moment, you can forget yourself—and there is no other way of forgetting yourself. Everything else you do in life gives emphasis to the 'me'.

Sex becomes an extraordinarily difficult and complex problem so long as you do not understand the mind which thinks about the problem. The act itself can never be a problem, but the thought about the act creates the problem. The act you safeguard; you live loosely, or indulge yourself in marriage, thereby making your wife into a prostitute, which is all apparently very respectable, and you are satisfied to leave it at that.

Surely the problem can be solved only when you understand the whole process and structure of the 'me' and the 'mine': my wife, my child, my property, my car, my achievement, my success; until you understand and resolve all that, sex as a problem will remain. So long as you are ambitious, politically, religiously, or in any way; so long as you are emphasizing the self, the thinker, the experiencer, by feeding him on ambition, whether in the name of yourself as an individual or in the name of the country, of the party, or of an idea which you call religion—so long as there is this activity of self-expansion, you will have a sexual problem.[48]

*F*IRST OF ALL WHY HAVE HUMAN BEINGS, right throughout the world, made sex so important in their life? Do you understand my question? Why? Now in the west it is permissive: boys or girls of twelve, thirteen, already have sex. And one asks why have human beings throughout their activities, throughout their lives made this thing of such colossal importance? Go on, answer it. Put the question. We are sharing the question together—right? You are not just listening to a Delphic Oracle, but together we are investigating. It is your life. We are looking at it.

There is a whole philosophy called tantra, part of which is based on sex, saying that through sex you can reach God—whatever that god be. That is very popular. And there are those, like the monks, the Indian sannyasis, and the Buddhist priests, who have denied sex because they have all maintained that it is a waste of energy, and to serve God you must come with all your energy. Therefore deny, suppress, burn inside yourself with all the demands but suppress it, control it.

So you have the permissive, and the so-called religious suppression. And those in between who enjoy everything, both sides, they have one foot in this and one foot in the other! Then they can talk about both things and see if they cannot harmonize the two together and find God—or whatever you want to find. Probably you will find, at the end of it, a lot of nonsense!

So we are asking: why has man, woman made this sex business so important? Why don't you give the same importance to love—do you understand? To compassion? Not to kill? Why do you give such immense value only to sex? Your wars, terrors, national divisions, the whole immoral society in which we live, why don't you give an equal importance to all that and not only to this?

Is it because sex is your greatest pleasure in life? The rest of your life is a bore, a travail, a struggle, a conflict, meaningless existence? And this at least gives you a certain sense of great pleasure, a sense of well-being, a sense of—you know—what you call relationship, and what you also call love, right? Is that the reason why we are so sexually crazy? Because we are not free in any other direction?

You have to go to the office from nine to five, where you are bullied, where your boss is over you—you know all that happens in an office, or in a factory, or in another job where there is somebody dominating you. And our minds have become mechanical; we repeat, repeat, repeat; we fall into a tradition, into a groove, into a rut. Our thinking is that: I am a Christian, I am a Buddhist, I am a Hindu, I am a Catholic—you know, the whole thing is clearly marked and you follow that. Or you reject all that and form your own routine.

So our minds have become slaves to various patterns of existence—right? So it has become mechanical. And sex may be pleasurable, and gradually that too becomes mechanical. So one asks—if you want to go very deeply into it—one asks: is love sex? Go on, ask it. Is love pleasure? Is love desire? Is love a remembrance of an incident, which you call sex, with all the imagination, the pictures, the thinking about it—is that love? Oh, for god's sake! Is love a remembrance?

You see what it is reduced to? Human relationship is pleasure, sex, conflict, quarrels, divisions—you go your way, I'll go my way—you follow? That is our relationship, actual relationship in our daily life. We are jealous of each other, we want to possess each other, we want to dominate each other, and so there is antagonism between each other, one is sexually unsatisfied, therefore you go to somebody else, and in that sexual relationship there is loneliness—right? All this, and always seeking your own pleasure, is that all love?

So you disregard, put aside that thing called love—perhaps that is the most wonderful thing if one has it—and are so caught up in this vortex of one's own desire, of one's own pleasure—right? So we are always wanting, not only sexual satisfaction, but gratification in every direction, which is based on pleasure. And that we call love. From love of a country we kill each other.

At the end of this, you ask why man, woman have given this one thing such extraordinary importance. Is it that man, woman have lost their creative capacity—not sexual capacity, creative capacity—to be able to see, to be a light to themselves, not to follow anybody, not to worship any image, illusion, belief?

When you put aside all that and you have understood your own petty little desires, which is your own sexual demands, gratifications—then when you see all that, have an insight into all that, out of that comes creation. It doesn't mean painting a picture, or writing a poem. That sense of ever freshness, you understand?—having a mind that is fresh, young, innocent all the time, not clouded, burdened with all kinds of memories, dissatisfactions, fears, and anxieties. You know, when you have lost all that, there is a totally different kind of mind. Then sex has its own place.

Apparently we don't have that quality of skepticism—you understand?—to be skeptical about one's own demands, to question, doubt.[49]

HAPPINESS

Questioner: Are we not really seeking happiness?

Krishnamurti: In answering this question, to understand it fully and significantly, should we not perhaps understand first this idea of seeking? Why are we seeking happiness? Why this incessant pursuit to be happy, to be joyous, to be something? Why is there this search, this immense effort made to find? If we can understand that and go into it fully, perhaps we shall know what happiness is, without seeking it.

Because, after all, happiness is a by-product—of secondary importance. It is not an end in itself; it has no meaning if it is an end in itself. What does it mean to be happy? The man who takes a drink is happy. The man who drops a bomb over a great number of people feels elated and says he is happy, or that God is with him. Momentary sensations, which disappear, give that sense of being happy.

Surely, there is some other quality that is essential for happiness. For happiness is not an end, any more than virtue. Virtue is not an end in itself; it gives freedom, and in that freedom there is discovery. Therefore, virtue is essential. Whereas, an unvirtuous person is slavish, is disorderly, is all over the place, lost, confused. But to treat virtue as an end in itself, or happiness as an end in itself, has very little meaning. So, happiness is not an end. It is a secondary issue, a by-product which will come into being if we understand something else. It is this understanding of something else, and not merely the search for happiness, that is important.[50]

SENSATION IS ONE THING, and happiness is another. Sensation is always seeking further sensation, ever in wider and wider circles. There is no end to the pleasures of sensa-

115

tion; they multiply, but there is always dissatisfaction in their fulfillment; there is always the desire for more, and the demand for more is without end. Sensation and dissatisfaction are inseparable, for the desire for more binds them together. Sensation is the desire for more and also the desire for less. In the very act of the fulfillment of sensation, the demand for more is born.

Mind can never find happiness. Happiness is not a thing to be pursued and found, as sensation. Sensation can be found again and again, for it is ever being lost; but happiness cannot be found. Remembered happiness is only a sensation, a reaction for or against the present. What is over is not happiness; the experience of happiness which is over is sensation, for remembrance is the past and the past is sensation. Happiness is not sensation.[51]

Questioner: What is happiness? Is it not the search for happiness that makes the mind crave for new experiences? Is there a state of happiness that is beyond the mind?

Krishnamurti: Why do we inquire "what is happiness"? Is that the right approach? Is that the right probing? We are not happy. If we were happy, our world would be entirely different; our civilization, our culture would be wholly, radically different. We are unhappy human beings, petty, miserable, struggling, vain, surrounding ourselves with useless, futile things, satisfied with petty ambitions, with money and position. We are unhappy beings, though we may have knowledge, though we may have money, rich houses, plenty of children, cars, experience.

We are unhappy suffering human beings, and because we are suffering, we want happiness, and so we are led away by those who promise this happiness, social, economic, or spiritual. So we want to escape from *what is*—the suffering, the pain, the loneliness, the despair. We want to run away from it, and the very running away gives us experience, and that experience we call happiness. Is there any other kind of happiness?

What is the good of my asking if there is happiness when I am suffering? Can I understand suffering? That is my problem, not how to be happy. I am happy when I am not suffering, but the moment I am conscious of it, it is not happiness. Is it not so? Because the moment I know I am virtuous, I cease to be virtuous. The moment I know I am humble, courageous, generous, the moment I am aware of it, then I am not that.

Happiness, like virtue, is not a thing to be sought after, not a thing to be invited. Virtue when cultivated becomes immoral because it strengthens the 'me', the 'I', leading to respectability, which is the self. So, I must understand what is suffering. Can I understand what is suffering when a part of my mind is running away seeking happiness, seeking a way out of this misery? Must I not—if I am to understand suffering—be completely one with it, not reject it, not justify it, not condemn it, not compare it but completely be with it and understand it?

Can I listen to the voice of suffering without projections? I cannot listen when I am seeking happiness. So my probing, my inquiry is no longer what is happiness, nor if there is happiness beyond my mind, nor whether it is permanent or impermanent, nor whether it is an experience and therefore to be stored. The moment I do any of these things, it is already gone; therefore it is no longer happiness. But the truth of what is happiness will come if I know how to listen. I must know how to listen to suffering; if I can listen to suffering I can listen to happiness because that is what I am.

I suffer; I am fearful of death; I desire to be secure after death; I desire to be permanent, to have position, wealth, comfort; I am filled with the ache of loneliness. So can I listen to all that? Then, my problem is no longer a way to happiness but to find out how to listen to the voice of suffering, just to listen without trying to interpret it. And that is a very arduous process because the mind continuously objects to living with suffering—to look at it, not to interpret it, not to justify it, not to translate it, not to condemn it, but to look at it, to know its content, to be acquainted with it, to love it. The mind is capable of listening to that voice which is beyond suffering, only when the mind is not running away from it into some futile imagination or illusion or some desire for satisfaction.

So what is important is not if there is happiness, but from the very beginning to inquire into what suffering is, and to stay with that until the right answer comes. The right answer cannot come if you are seeking. The moment you search for the right answer, the mind is projecting because it wants the answer; therefore it is not concerned with listening to suffering. It is not concerned with listening, but it is concerned with the answer which will reject this suffering.

The moment you wish to reject something, then you will find an answer which will be satisfactory, and so it will be that satisfaction which the mind seeks and not the understanding of suffering. After all, that is what we all want. We want satisfaction, either in a position, in relationship, or in ideas. And the more we are satisfied, the more the suffering. Because, the mind that is satisfied is never let alone; it is always being challenged on every side of life.

So a mind realizing that it is seeking satisfaction—the very desire to find an answer for suffering is to be satisfied—totally puts aside all this. Therefore it is only listening, seeing the whole process of how the mind runs away, how it never can stay with suffering—such as facing fear. Fear comes only when you are running away from it. Fear exists in the process of flight, not when you are confronted with the thing. It is only when you are running away from the thing, in the very running away, fear is created—not when you are watching the thing, the *what is*.

So, similarly, can I look at suffering without running away—which creates sorrow, which creates fear, which prevents me from looking at it? If I can look at it, then there is a possibility of listening to suffering without interpretation, without judgment, without translating or asking for a result. Then only is there a possibility of listening, of trying to find something beyond the mind.

We cannot find what is beyond the mind if we do not know, if we are incapable of facing *what is*. And it requires enormous attention, great passive awareness to observe without justification, without judgment, just to observe, just to listen. In that, there is transformation. In that, there is happiness which is not measured by time, by the mind.[52]

WHEN YOU SEE A BEAUTIFUL THING, there is immediate joy; you see a sunset and there is an immediate reaction of joy. That joy, a few moments later, becomes a memory. That memory of the joy, is it a living thing? Is the memory of the sunset a living thing? No, it is a dead thing. So, with that dead imprint of a sunset, through that, you want to find joy.

Memory has no joy; it is only the remembrance of something which created the joy. Memory in itself has no joy. There is joy, the immediate reaction to the beauty of a tree; and then memory comes in and destroys that joy. So, if there is constant perception of beauty without the accumulation of memories, then there is the possibility of joy everlasting.

But it is not so easy to be free from memory. The moment you see something very pleasurable, you make it immediately into something to which you hold on. You see a beautiful thing, a beautiful child, a beautiful tree; and when you see it, there is immediate pleasure; then you want more of it. The more of it is the reaction of memory. So, when you want more, you have already started the process of disintegration.[53]

JOY IS NOT PLEASURE. You can't think about joy; you can think about it and reduce it to pleasure, but the thing that is called joy, ecstasy, is not the product of thought. Haven't you noticed when there is a great burst of joy, you can't think about it the next day; and if you do, it has already become pleasure?

So, fear and pleasure are sustained by thought, given continuity by thought. How is one to look at great beauty—the beauty of a cloudless sky, the beauty of a sunset, the beauty of a face, the beauty of truth—to look at it and end it, and not think about it?

We carry our pleasures and our fears. As a human being, you, the self, the 'me', is the burden of the fear and the pleasure. And you are afraid to lose that burden. A mind that understands the nature and the structure of thought is free of fear. And because it understands fear, it understands also pleasure, which doesn't mean that you cannot have pleasure. When you look at a cloud and a leaf, it is a pleasure to look; the beauty of anything is a pleasure, but to carry it to the next day, then pain begins.

Joy is something entirely different from pleasure. You can invite pleasure, you can think about it, sustain it, nourish it, seek it out, pursue it, hold it; but you cannot with joy, with ecstasy. And that happens naturally, easily, without any invitation, this ecstasy, when you understand fear and pleasure.

A mind that is really free of this—or rather understands it—then such a mind which is with ecstasy, is never violent, is never ambitious, never seeking position, prestige, and all the rest of that nonsense.54

THERE IS NO DUALITY IN ECSTASY. It is a state which spontaneously comes into being without our willing it. Suffering is an indication of duality. Without understanding this, we perpetuate duality through the many intellectual efforts and processes of overcoming it, giving oneself over to its opposite, developing virtues, and so forth. All such attempts only strengthen duality.

If there is a lack of sensibility to ugliness, to sorrow, there must also be deep insensitiveness to beauty, to joy. Resistance against sorrow is also a barrier to happiness.

What is ecstasy? That state of being when the mind and heart are in complete union, when fear does not tear them asunder, when the mind is not withholding.55

YOU CANNOT, MAY NOT INVITE JOY; if you do, it becomes pleasure. Pleasure is the movement of thought and thought may not, can in no way cultivate joy, and if it pursues that which has been joyous, then it's only a remembrance, a dead thing. Beauty is never time-binding; it is wholly free of time and so of culture. It is there when the self is not. The self is put together by time, by the movement of thought, by the known, by the word. In the abandonment of the self, in that total attention, that essence of beauty is there. The letting go of the self is not the calculated action of desire-will. Will is directive and so resistant, divisive, and so breeds conflict. The dissolution of the self is not the evolution of the knowledge of the self; time as a factor does not enter into it at all. There is no way or means to end it. The total inward nonaction is the positive attention of beauty.[56]

WHEN YOU LOOK AT A CLOUD, at the light in that cloud, there is beauty. Beauty is passion. To see the beauty of a cloud or the beauty of light on a tree, there must be passion, there must be intensity. In this intensity, this passion, there is no sentiment whatsoever, no feeling of like or dislike. Ecstasy is not personal; ecstasy is not yours or mine, just as love is not yours or mine.[57]

Self
and
Identification

SELF AND
IDENTIFICATION

*E*XPERIENCE NEARLY ALWAYS FORMS a hardened center in the mind, as the self, which is a deteriorating factor. Most of us are seeking experience. We may be tired of the worldly experiences of fame, notoriety, wealth, sex, and so on, but we all want greater, wider experience of some kind. We think the pursuit of experience is the right way of life in order to attain greater vision, and I question whether that is so.

Does this search for experience, which is really a demand for greater, fuller sensation, lead to reality? Or is it a factor which cripples the mind? Through it all, the fundamental desire is for greater sensation—to have the sensation of pleasure extended, made high and permanent, as opposed to the suffering, the dullness, the routine and loneliness of our daily lives.

So the mind is ever seeking experience, and that experience hardens into a center, and from this center we act. We live and have our being in this center, in this accumulated, hardened experience of the past. And is it possible to live without forming this center of experience and sensation? Because it seems to me that life will then have a significance quite different from that which we now give it. At present we are all concerned, are we not, with the extension of the center, recruiting greater and wider experience which ever strengthens the self, and I think this invariably limits the mind.

So, is it possible to live in this world without forming this center? I think it is possible only when there is a full awareness of life—an awareness in which there is no motive or choice, but simple observation. I think you will find, if you will experiment with this and think about it a little deeply, that such awareness does not form a center around which experience and the reactions to experience can accumulate. Then the mind becomes astonishingly alive, creative—and I do not mean writing poems or painting pictures but a creativeness in which the self is totally absent. I think this is what most of us are really seeking—a state in which there is no conflict, a state of peace and serenity of mind. But this is not possible so long as the mind is the instrument of sensation and is ever demanding further sensation.

After all, most of our memory is based on sensation, either pleasurable or painful; from the painful we try to escape, and to the pleasurable we cling; the one we suppress or seek to avoid, and the other we grope after, hold on to, and think about. So the center of our experience is essentially based on pleasure and pain, which are sensations, and we are always pursuing experiences which we hope will be permanently satisfying. That is what we are after all the time, and hence there is everlasting conflict.

Conflict is never creative; on the contrary, conflict is a most destructive factor, both within the mind itself and in our relationship with the world around us, which is society. If we can understand this really deeply—that a mind which seeks experience limits itself and is its own source of misery—then perhaps we can find out what it is to be aware.

Being aware does not mean learning and accumulating lessons from life; on the contrary, to be aware is to be without the scars of accumulated experience. After all, when the mind merely gathers experience according to its own wishes, it remains very shallow, superficial. A mind which is deeply observant does not get caught up in self-centered activities, and the mind is not observant if there is any action of condemnation or comparison. Comparison and condemnation do not bring understanding, rather they block understanding. To be aware is to observe—just to observe—without any self-identifying process. Such a mind is free of that hard core which is formed by self-centered activities.

I think it is very important to experience this state of awareness for oneself, and not merely to know about it through any description which another may give. Awareness comes into being naturally, easily, spontaneously, when we understand the center which is everlastingly seeking experience, sensation. A mind which seeks sensation through experience becomes insensitive, incapable of swift movement, and therefore it is never free. But in understanding its own self-centered activities, the mind comes upon this state of awareness which is choiceless, and such a mind is then capable of complete silence, stillness.[58]

I WOULD LIKE TO DISCUSS how experience strengthens the self.

You know what I mean by the self? By that, I mean the idea, the memory, the conclusion, the experience, the various forms of nameable and unnameable intentions, the conscious endeavor to be or not to be, the accumulated memory of the unconscious, the racial, the group, the individual, the clan, and the whole of it all, whether it is projected outwardly in action, or projected spiritually as virtue; the striving after all this is the self. In it is included the competition, the desire to be.

The whole process of that is the self; and we know actually when we are faced with it, that it is an evil thing. I am using the word *evil* intentionally, because the self is dividing; the self is self-enclosing; its activities, however noble, are separated and isolated. We know all this. We also know that extraordinary are the moments when the self is not there, in which there is no sense of endeavor, of effort, and which happens when there is love.

It seems to me that it is important to understand how experience strengthens the self. If we are earnest, we should understand this problem of experience.

Now, what do we mean by experience? We have experiences all the time, impressions; and we translate those impressions, and we are reacting to them; or we are acting according to those impressions; we are calculated, cunning, and so on. There is the constant interplay between what is seen objectively and our reacting to it, and the interplay between the unconscious and the memories of the unconscious.

According to my memories, I react to whatever I see, to whatever I feel. In this process of reacting to what I see, what I feel, what I know, what I believe, experience is taking place. Is it not? Reaction to the response of something seen is experience. When I see you, I react; the reaction is experience. The naming of that reaction is experience. If I do not name that reaction, it is not an experience. Please do watch it. Watch your own responses and what is taking place about you. There is no experience unless there is a naming process going on at the same time. If I do not recognize you, how can I have experience?

Then there is the projection of various desires. I desire to be protected, to have security inwardly; or I desire to have a Master, a guru, a teacher, a god; and I experience that which I have projected. That is, I have projected a desire, which has taken a form, to which I have given a name; to that, I react. It is my projection. It is my naming. That desire which gives me an experience, makes me say: "I have got," "I have experienced," "I have met the Master," or "I have not met the Master." You know the whole process of naming an experience. Desire is what you call experience. Is it not?

When I desire silence of the mind, what is taking place? What happens? I see the importance of having a silent mind, a quiet mind, for various reasons. I want to have a silent mind, and so I ask you how to get it. I know what this book or that book says about meditation and the various forms of discipline. I want a silent mind through discipline and I experience silence. The self, the 'me', has established itself in the experience of silence. Am I making myself clear?

I want to understand what is truth; that is my desire, my longing; then there is my projection of what I consider to be the truth, because I have read lots about it; I have heard many people talk about it; religious scriptures have described it. I want all that. What happens? The very want, the very desire is projected and I experience because I recognize that state. If I do not recognize that state, that act, that truth, I would not call it truth. I recognize it and I experience it. That experience gives strength to the self, to the 'me'.

So experience is always strengthening the 'me'. The more you are strengthened, the more entrenched you are in your experience and the more does the self get strengthened. As a result of this, you have a certain strength of character, strength of knowledge, of belief, which you put across to other people because you know they are not so clever as you are, and because you have the gift of the pen and you are cunning.

Because the self is still acting, your beliefs, your Masters, your castes, your economic system are all a process of isolation, and they therefore bring contention. You must, if you are at all serious or earnest in this, dissolve this completely and not justify it. That is why we must understand the process of experience.

Is it possible for the mind, for the self, not to project, not to desire, not to experience? We see all experiences of the self are a negation, a destruction; and yet, we call the same a positive action. Don't we? That is what we call the positive way of life. To undo this whole process is what you call negation. Are you right in that? There is nothing positive. Can we, you and I as individuals, go to the root of it and understand the process of the self?

Now what is the element that dissolves it? What brings about dissolution of the self? Religious and other groups have explained it by identification. Have they not? Identify yourself with a larger, and the self disappears; that is what they say. We say here that identification is still the process of the self; the larger is simply the projection of the 'me', which I experience and which therefore strengthens the 'me'. I wonder if you are following this. All the various forms of discipline, beliefs, and knowledge only strengthen the self.

Can we find an element which would dissolve the self? Or, is that a wrong question? That is what we want basically. We want to find some thing which will dissolve the 'me'. Is it not? We think there are various forms of finding that—

namely, identification, belief, etc.; but, all of them are at the same level; one is not superior to the other, because all of them are equally powerful in strengthening the self, the 'me'.

Now, I see the 'me' wherever it functions, and I see its destructive forces and energy. Whatever name you may give to it, it is an isolating force, it is a destructive force; and I want to find a way of dissolving it. You must have asked this yourself: I see the 'I' functioning all the time and always bringing anxiety, fear, frustration, despair, misery, not only to myself but to all around me. Is it possible for that self to be dissolved, not partially but completely? Can we go to the root of it and destroy it? That is the only way of functioning. Is it not?

I do not want to be partially intelligent but intelligent in an integrated manner. Most of us are intelligent in layers, you probably in one way, and I in some other way. Some of you are intelligent in your business work, some others in your office work, and so on; people are intelligent in different ways; but, we are not integrally intelligent. To be integrally intelligent means to be without the self. Is it possible? If I pursue that action, what is your response? The implications which I have tried to point out must produce a reaction in you. What is your response?

Is it possible for the self now to be completely absent? You know it is possible. Now, how is it possible? What are the necessary ingredients, requirements? What is the element that brings it about? Can I find it? When I put that question "Can I find it?" surely, I am convinced that it is possible. I have already created an experience in which the self is going to be strengthened. Is it not? I who am very earnest, want to dissolve the self. Then I say that I know it is possible to dissolve the self. The moment I say, "I want to dissolve this," in the process I follow for the dissolution of that, there is the experiencing of the self; and so, the self is strengthened.

Is it possible for the mind to be quite still, in a state of nonrecognition, which is, nonexperiencing, to be in a state in which creation can take place, which means, when the self is not there, when the self is absent?

The problem is this, is it not? Any movement of the mind, positive or negative, is an experience which actually strengthens the 'me'. Is it possible for the mind not to recognize? That can only take place when there is complete silence, but not the silence which is an experience of the self, and which therefore strengthens the self.

Is there an entity apart from the self, which looks at the self and dissolves the self? Are you following all this? Is there a spiritual entity which supersedes the self and destroys it, which puts it aside? We think there is. Don't we? Most religious people think there is such an element.

The materialist says: "It is impossible for the self to be destroyed; it can only be conditioned and restrained—politically, economically, and socially; we can hold it firmly within a certain pattern and we can break it; and therefore it can be made to lead a high life, a moral life, and not to interfere with anything but to follow the social pattern, and to function merely as a machine." That, we know.

There are other people, the so-called religious ones—they are not really religious, though we call them so—who say "Fundamentally, there is such an element. If we can get into touch with it, it will dissolve the self."

Is there such an element to dissolve the self? Please see what we are doing. We are merely forcing the self into a corner. If you allow yourself to be forced into the corner, you will see what is going to happen. We would like that there should be an element which is timeless, which is not of the self, which, we hope, will come and intercede and destroy, which we call God.

Now is there such a thing which the mind can conceive? There may be or there may not be; that is not the point. When the mind seeks a timeless spiritual state which will go into action in order to destroy the self, is that not another form of experience which is strengthening the 'me'? When you believe, is that not what is actually taking place? When you believe that there is truth, God, timeless state, immortality, is that not the process of strengthening the self?

The self has projected that thing which you feel and believe will come and destroy the self. So, having projected

130

this idea of continuance in a timeless state as spiritual entity, you are going to experience; and all such experience will only strengthen the self; and therefore what have you done? You have not really destroyed the self but only given it a different name, a different quality; the self is still there because you have experienced it. So, our action from the beginning to the end is the same action; only we think it is evolving, growing, becoming more and more beautiful; but, if you observe inwardly, it is the same action going on, the same 'me' functioning at different levels with different labels, with different names.

When you see the whole process, the cunning, extraordinary inventions, the intelligence of the self—how it covers itself up through identification, through virtue, through experience, through belief, through knowledge—when you see that you are moving in a circle, in a cage of its own making, what happens? When you are aware of it, fully cognizant of it, then, is not your mind extraordinarily quiet—not through compulsion, not through any reward, not through any fear?

When you recognize that every movement of the mind is merely a form of strengthening the self, when you observe it, see it, when you are completely aware of it in action, when you come to that point—not ideologically, verbally, not through experiencing, but when you are actually in that state—then you will see that the mind, being utterly still, has no power of creating. Whatever the mind creates is in a circle, within the field of the self. When the mind is noncreating, there is creation, which is not a recognizable process.

Reality, truth, is not to be recognized. For truth to come, belief, knowledge, experiencing, virtue, pursuit of virtue—which is different from being virtuous—all this must go.

The virtuous person who is conscious of pursuing virtue can never find reality. He may be a very decent person; that is entirely different from the man of truth, from the man who understands. To the man of truth, truth has come into being. A virtuous man is a righteous man, and a righteous man can never understand what is truth because virtue to him is the covering of the self, the strengthening of the self, because he is pursuing virtue. When he says, "I must be without greed," the state in which he is nongreedy and which he experiences, strengthens the self.

That is why it is so important to be poor, not only in the things of the world, but also in belief and in knowledge. A rich man with worldly riches, or a man rich in knowledge and belief will never know anything but darkness, and will be the center of all mischief and misery. But if you and I, as individuals, can see this whole working of the self, then we shall know what love is. I assure you that is the only reformation which can possibly change the world. Love is not the self. Self cannot recognize love. You say, "I love," but then, in the very saying of it, in the very experiencing of it, love is not. But, when you know love, self is not. When there is love, self is not.[59]

OUR SOCIAL AND RELIGIOUS STRUCTURE is based on the urge to become something, positively or negatively. Such a process is the very nourishment of the ego, through name, family, achievement, through identification of the me and mine which is ever causing conflict and sorrow. We perceive the results of this way of life: strife, confusion, and antagonism, ever spreading, ever engulfing. How is one to transcend strife and sorrow? This is what we are attempting to understand during these discussions.

Is not craving the very root of the self? How is thought, which has become the means of self-expansion, to act without giving sustenance to the ego, the cause of conflict and sorrow? Is this not an important question? Do not let me make it important to you. Is this not a vital question to each one? If it is, must we not find the true answer? We are nourishing the ego in many ways, and before we condemn or encourage we must understand its significance, must we not?

We use religion and philosophy as a means of self-expansion; our social structure is based on the aggrandizement of the self; the clerk will become the manager and later the owner, the pupil will become the Master and so on. In

132

this process there is ever conflict, antagonism, sorrow. Is this an intelligent and inevitable process? We can discover truth for ourselves only when we do not depend on another; no specialist can give us the right answer. Each one has to find the right answer directly for himself. For this reason it is important to be earnest.

We vary in our earnestness according to circumstances, our moods and fancies. Earnestness must be independent of circumstances and moods, of persuasion and hope. We often think that perhaps through shock we shall be made earnest, but dependence is never productive of earnestness. Earnestness comes into being with inquiring awareness, and are we so alertly aware?

If you are aware, you will realize that your mind is constantly engaged in the activities of the ego and its identification; if you pursue this activity further, you will find the deep-seated self-interest. These thoughts of self-interest arise from the needs of daily life, things you do from moment to moment, your role in society and so on, all of which build up the structure of the ego.

This seems so strangely inevitable, but before we accept this inevitability, must we not be aware of our purposive intention: whether we desire to nourish the ego or not? For according to our hidden intentions, we will act. We know how the self is built up and strengthened through the pleasure and pain principle, through memory, through identification and so on. This process is the cause of conflict and sorrow. Do we earnestly seek to put an end to the cause of sorrow?

Through being choicelessly aware of your intentions, the truth of the matter is known. We are often blocked because unconsciously we are afraid to take action, which might lead to further trouble and suffering. But no clear and definite action can take place if we have not uncovered our deep and hidden intention with regard to nourishing and maintaining the self.

Is not this fear, which hinders understanding, the result of projection, speculation? You imagine that freedom from self-expansion is a state of nothingness, an emptiness, and this creates fear, thus preventing any actual experience. Through speculation, through imagination you prevent the discovery of *what is*. As the self is in constant flux we seek, through identification, permanency. Identification brings about the illusion of permanency, and it is the loss of this which causes fear.

We recognize that the self is in constant flux; yet, we cling to something which we call the permanent in the self, an enduring self which we fabricate out of the impermanent self. If we deeply experienced and understood that the self is ever impermanent, then there would be no identification with any particular form of craving, with any particular country, nation, or with any organized system of thought or religion, for with identification comes the horror of war, the ruthlessness of so-called civilization.[60]

MANY OF US HAVE EXPERIENCED, at one time or another, that state when the 'me', the self, with its aggressive demands, has completely ceased, and the mind is extraordinarily quiet, without any direct volition—that state wherein, perhaps, one may experience something that is without measure, something that it is impossible to put into words.

There must have been these rare moments when the self, the 'me', with all its memories and travails, with all its anxieties and fears, has completely ceased. One is then a being without any motive, without any compulsion; and in that state one feels or is aware of an astonishing sense of immeasurable distance, of limitless space and being.

This must have happened to many of us. And I think it would be worthwhile if we could go into this question together and see whether it is possible to resolve the enclosing, limiting self, this restricting 'me' that worries, that has anxieties, fears, that is dominating and dominated, that has innumerable memories, that is cultivating virtue and trying in every way to become something, to be important.

I do not know if you have noticed the constant effort that one is consciously or unconsciously making to express oneself, to be something, either socially, morally, or economically.

This entails, does it not, a great deal of striving. Our whole life is based on the everlasting struggle to arrive, to achieve, to become.

The more we struggle, the more significant and exaggerated the self becomes, with all its limitations, fears, ambitions, frustrations; and there must have been times when each one has asked himself whether it is not possible to be totally without the self.

After all, we do have rare moments when the sense of the self is not. I am not talking of the transmutation of the self to a higher level, but of the simple cessation of the 'me' with its anxieties, worries, fears—the absence of the self. One realizes that such a thing is possible, and then one sets about deliberately, consciously, to eliminate the self. After all, that is what organized religions try to do—to help each worshipper, each believer, to lose himself in something greater, and thereby perhaps to experience some higher state.

If you are not a so-called religious person, then you identify yourself with the State, with the country, and try to lose yourself in that identification, which gives you the feeling of greatness, of being something much larger than the petty little self, and all the rest of it. Or, if we do not do that, we try to lose ourselves in social work of some kind, again with the same intention.

We think that if we can forget ourselves, deny ourselves, put ourselves out of the way by dedicating our lives to something much greater and more vital than ourselves, we shall perhaps experience a bliss, a happiness which is not merely a physical sensation. And if we do none of these things, we hope to stop thinking about ourselves through the cultivation of virtue, through discipline, through control, through constant practice.

Now, I do not know if you have thought about it, but all this implies, surely, a ceaseless effort to be or become something. And perhaps, in listening to what is being said, we can together go into this whole process and discover for ourselves whether it is possible to wipe away the sense of the 'me' without this fearful, restricting discipline, without this enormous effort to deny ourselves, this constant struggle to renounce our wants, our ambitions, in order to be something or to achieve some reality. I think in this lies the real issue. Because all effort implies motive, does it not? I make an effort to forget myself in something, in some ritual or ideology, because in thinking about myself I am unhappy. When I think about something else, I am more relaxed, my mind is quieter, I seem to feel better, I look at things differently. So I make an effort to forget myself. But behind my effort there is a motive, which is to escape from myself because I suffer; and that motive is essentially a part of the self.

Now, is it possible to forget oneself without any motive? Because, we can see very well that any motive has within it the seed of the self, with its anxiety, ambition, frustration, its fear of not being, and the immense urge to be secure. And can all that fall away easily, without any effort? Which means, really, can you and I, as individuals, live in this world without being identified with anything?

After all, I identify myself with my country, with my religion, with my family, with my name, because without identification I am nothing. Without a position, without power, without prestige of one kind or another, I feel lost; and so I identify myself with my name, with my family, with my religion, I join some organization or become a monk—we all know the various types of identification that the mind clings to. But can we live in this world without any identification at all?

If we can think about this, if we can listen to what is being said and at the same time be aware of our own intimations regarding the implications of identification, then I think we shall discover, if we are at all serious, that it is possible to live in this world without the nightmare of identification and the ceaseless struggle to achieve a result.

Then, I think, knowledge has quite a different significance. At present we identify ourselves with our knowledge and use it as a means of self-expansion, just as we do with the nation, with a religion, or with some activity. Identification with the knowledge we have gained is another way of furthering the self, is it not? Through knowledge the 'me' continues its struggle to be something, and thereby perpetuates misery, pain.

If we can very humbly and simply see the implications of all this, be aware, without assuming anything, of how our minds operate and what our thinking is based on, then I think we shall realize the extraordinary contradiction that exists in this whole process of identification.

After all, it is because I feel empty, lonely, miserable that I identify myself with my country, and this identification gives me a sense of well-being, a feeling of power. Or, for the same reason, I identify myself with a hero, with a saint. But if I can go into this process of identification very deeply, then I will see that the whole movement of my thinking and all my activity, however noble, is essentially based on the continuance of myself in one form or another.

Now, if I once see that, if I realize it, feel it with my whole being, then religion has quite a different meaning. Then religion is no longer a process of identifying myself with God, but rather the coming into being of a state in which there is only that reality, and not the 'me'. But this cannot be a mere verbal assertion, it is not just a phrase to be repeated.

That is why it is very important, it seems to me, to have self-knowledge, which means going very deeply into oneself without assuming anything, so that the mind has no deceptions, no illusions, so that it does not trick itself into visions and false states. Then, perhaps, it is possible for the enclosing process of the self to come to an end—but not through any form of compulsion or discipline; because the more you discipline the self, the stronger the self becomes.

What is important is to go into all this very deeply and patiently, without taking anything for granted, so that one begins to understand the ways, the purposes, the motives and directions of the mind. Then, I think, the mind comes to a state in which there is no identification at all, and therefore no effort to be something; then there is the cessation of the self, and I think that is the real.

Although we may swiftly, fleetingly experience this state, the difficulty for most of us is that the mind clings to the experience and wants more of it; and the very wanting of more is again the beginning of the self. That is why it is very important, for those of us who are really serious in these matters, to be inwardly aware of the process of our own thinking, to silently observe our motives, our emotional reactions, and not merely say, "I know myself very well"—for actually one does not.

You may know your reactions and motives superficially, at the conscious level. But the self, the 'me', is a very complex affair, and to go into the totality of the self needs persistent and continuous inquiry without a motive, without an end in view.

We follow because we want to be secure, whether economically, socially, or religiously. After all, the mind is always seeking security, it wants to be safe in this world, and also in the next world. That is why we create the authority of the government, the dictator, and the authority of the church, the idol, the image. So long as we follow, we must create authority, and that authority becomes ultimately evil because we have thoughtlessly given ourselves over to domination by another.

I think it is important to go deeply into this whole question and begin to understand why the mind insists on following. You follow not only political and religious leaders but also what you read in the newspapers, in magazines, in books; you seek the authority of the specialists, the authority of the written word. All this indicates—does it not?—that the mind is uncertain of itself. One is afraid to think apart from what has been said by the leaders because one might lose one's job, be ostracized, excommunicated, or put into a concentration camp.

We submit to authority because all of us have this inward demand to be safe, this urge to be secure. So long as we want to be secure—in our possessions, in our power, in our thoughts—we must have authority, we must be followers; and in that lies the seed of evil, for it invariably leads to the exploitation of man by man. He who would really find out what truth is, what God is, can have no authority, whether of the book, of the government, of the image, or of the priest; he must be totally free of all that.

This is very difficult for most of us because it means being insecure, standing completely alone, searching, groping, never being satisfied, never seeking success. But if we seriously experiment with it, then I think we shall find that there is no longer any question of creating or following authority, because something else begins to operate which is not a mere verbal statement but an actual fact. The man who is ceaselessly questioning, who has no authority, who does not follow any tradition, any book or teacher, becomes a light unto himself.

Merely to say: "Yes, I know myself very well" is just a superficial remark. But to realize, to actually experience that your whole being is nothing but a bundle of memories, that all your thinking, your reactions are mechanical is not at all easy. It means being aware, not only of the workings of the conscious mind, but also of the unconscious residue, the racial impressions, memories, the things that we have learned; it means discovering the whole field of the mind, the hidden as well as the visible, and that is extremely arduous.

And if my mind is merely the residue of the past, if it is only a bundle of memories, impressions, shaped by so-called education and various other influences, then is there any part of me which is not all that? Because, if I am merely a repeating machine, as most of us are—repeating what we have learned, what we have gathered, passing on what has been told to us—then any thought arising within this conditioned field obviously can only lead to further conditioning, further misery and limitation.

So, can the mind, knowing its limitation, being aware of its conditioning, go beyond itself? That is the problem. Merely to assert that it can, or it cannot, would be silly. Surely it is fairly obvious that the whole mind is conditioned. We are all conditioned—by tradition, by family, by experience, through the process of time. If you believe in God, that belief is the outcome of a particular conditioning, just as is the disbelief of the man who says he does not believe in God. So belief and disbelief have very little importance. But what is important is to understand the whole field of thought, and to see if the mind can go beyond it all.[61]

Krishnamurti: We are selfish entities. We are self-centered human beings, we think about ourselves, our worries, our family—we are the center. We can move the center to social work, to political work, but it is still the center operating.

Pupul Jayakar: That is a little more subtle to see, because you can concern yourself with something in which you feel the center is not involved.

K: You may think so. It is 'I' who work for the poor, but I am still working within this limitation.

PJ: Sir, I want some clarification. It is not the work for the poor which you are questioning?

K: No. It is the identification of myself with the poor, my identification of myself with the nation, identification of myself with God, identification of myself with some ideal and so on, that is the problem.

PJ: It is really like this: we have done everything to understand the nature of this self-centered activity. We have observed, we have meditated, but the center does not cease, sir.

K: No, because I think we are making a mistake. We don't actually see, perceive in our heart, in our mind, that any action within this periphery, from the center to the periphery, the circumference, and then from the circumference to the center, this movement back and forth, is a wastage of energy and must be limited and must bring sorrow. Everything within that area is sorrow. We don't see that.

PJ: Sir, if it is part of our brain cells and if it is the action of our brain cells to constantly throw out these ripples which get caught, which is in a sense self-centered existence, then—

K: No, Pupul, the brain needs two things: security and a sense of permanency.

PJ: Both are provided by the self.

K: That is why it has become very important.[62]

I AM ONLY CONSCIOUS OF THIS ACTIVITY OF THE 'ME' when I am opposing, when consciousness is thwarted, when the 'me' is desirous of achieving a result. The 'me' is active, or I am conscious of that center when pleasure comes to an end and I want to have more of that pleasure; then there is resistance and there is a purposive shaping of the mind to a particular end which will give me a delight, a satisfaction; I am aware of myself and my activities when I am pursuing virtue consciously. That is all we know. A man who pursues virtue consciously is unvirtuous. Humility cannot be pursued, and that is the beauty of humility.

So, as long as this center of activity in any direction, conscious and unconscious, exists, there is this movement of time, and I am conscious of the past and the present in conjunction with the future. The center of this activity, the self-centered activity of the 'me', is a time process. That is what you mean by time; you mean the psychological process of time; it is memory that gives continuity to the activity of the center which is the 'me'.

Please watch yourselves in operation; don't listen to my words or be mesmerized by my words. If you watch yourself and are aware of this center of activity, you will see that it is only the process of time, of memory, of experiencing and translating every experience according to memory; you also see that self-activity is recognition, which is the process of the mind.

Is it possible for the mind ever to be free from self-centered activity? That is a very important question first to put to ourselves, because in the very putting of it, you will find the answer. That is, if you are aware of the total process of this self-centered activity, fully cognizant of its activities at different levels of your consciousness, then surely you have to ask yourselves if it is possible for that activity to come to an end—that is, not to think in terms of time, not to think in terms of what I will be, what I have been, what I am.

From such thought, the whole process of self-centered activity begins; there also begin the determination to become, the determination to choose and to avoid, which are all a process of time. We see, in that process, infinite mischief, misery, confusion, distortion, deterioration taking place. Be aware of it as I am talking, in your relationship, in your mind.

Surely the process of time is not revolutionary. In the process of time, there is no transformation; there is only a continuity and no ending. In the process of time, there is nothing but recognition. It is only when you have complete cessation of the time process, of the activity of the self, is there the new, is there revolution, is there transformation.

Being aware of this whole total process of the 'me' in its activity, what is the mind to do? It is only with the renewal, it is only with the revolution—not through evolution, not through the 'me' becoming, but through the 'me' completely coming to an end—there is the new. The time process can't bring the new; time is not a way of creation.

I do not know if any of you have had a moment of creativity, not action—I am not talking of putting something into action—I mean that moment of creation when there is no recognition. At that moment, there is that extraordinary state in which the 'me', as an activity through recognition, has ceased. I think some of us have had it; perhaps, most of us have had it.

If we are aware, we will see in that state that there is no experiencer who remembers, translates, recognizes, and then identifies; there is no thought process which is of time. In

142

that state of creation, creativity, or in that state of the new, which is timeless, there is no action of the 'me' at all.

Now, our question surely is: Is it possible for the mind to experience, to have that state, not momentarily, not at rare moments but—I would not use the word *everlasting* or *forever*, because that would imply time—to have that state, to be in that state without regard to time?

Surely, that is an important discovery to be made by each one of us, because that is the door to love; all other doors are activities of the self. Where there is action of the self, there is no love. Love is not of time. You can't practice love. If you do, then it is a self-conscious activity of the 'me' which hopes through living to gain a result.

So, love is not of time; you can't come upon it through any conscious effort, through any discipline, through identification, which are all a process of time. The mind, knowing only the process of time, cannot recognize love. Love is the only thing that is new, eternally new. Since most of us have cultivated the mind, which is a process of time, which is the result of time, we do not know what love is. We talk about love; we say we love people, love our children, our wives, our neighbor; we say we love nature; but the moment I am conscious that I love, self-activity has come into being; therefore it ceases to be love.

This total process of the mind is to be understood only through relationship—relationship with nature, with people, with our own projection, with everything. In fact, life is nothing but relationship. Though we may attempt to isolate ourselves from relationship, we cannot exist without relationship; though relationship is painful, from which we try to run away through isolation by becoming a hermit and so on, we cannot do that.

All these methods are an indication of the activity of the self. Seeing this whole picture, being aware of this whole process of time as consciousness, without any choice, without any determined, purposive intention, without the desire for any result, you will see that this process of time comes to an end voluntarily, not induced, not as a result of desire. It is only when that process comes to an end that love is, which is eternally new.

We do not have to seek truth. Truth is not something far away. It is the truth of the mind, truth of its activities from moment to moment. If we are aware of this moment-to-moment truth, of this whole process of time, this awareness releases consciousness or that energy to be.

As long as the mind uses consciousness as the self-activity, time comes into being with all its miseries, with all its conflicts, with all its mischiefs, its purposive deceptions; and it is only when the mind, understanding this total process, ceases, that love will be. You may call it love or give it some other name; what name you give is of no consequence.[63]

THE SELF PERPETUATES THROUGH IDENTIFICATION, doesn't it? My son, my wife, my house, my furniture. My troubles, my anxieties, me, and all the rest of it. The identification with something perpetuates the 'me'. I identify myself with the furniture; because my furniture is very old, fourteenth century, I love it; I keep it very carefully, polish it, look after it; I value it because one day I will sell it, and I will get lots of money. So, the furniture has become more important than the 'me'. See the tricks which we are playing on ourselves and each other. Through identification with that, that becomes important, not the 'me' which identifies itself. I identify myself with my country, with my nationality, with my god. The country, the nationality, the god becomes all important.

We never inquire why this identification takes place. Why do I want to identify? I am asking the question—you have to ask the question.

I want to understand myself. I don't know what I am; I really don't know. I must find out. I must learn about myself, and not according to somebody else. Not according to the professionals; they may be wrong or they may be right. I am not concerned with them. I am concerned to learn about myself. To learn means I must observe, I must not come to it with any conclusion, with any prejudice, with any kind of hope. I must learn, find out what it is. Will you do that? People have said so many things about it. I discard everything the others have said. Will you do that? Discard completely what others have said.

I want to find out, so I look, I observe; I can observe that only in relationship: how I react, anger, jealousy, hate, envy, violence, domination, suppression; you know, the whole movement, I watch.

When you look at something, at a tree or a cloud, a mountain or water, you look at it with space, space between you and it. There is not only physical space but space divided by thought. That tree is in my garden. There is this division.

Can you look at that tree without that division? This doesn't mean you identify yourself with the tree, you don't become the tree. You observe it and in that observation, if there is no space between the observer and the observed, it is not identification but a totally different kind of relationship.

You do it sometime. To look at an object, it doesn't matter what it is, without the intervening space, then there is a direct contact. You can do that with a tree fairly easily. But, to do it with your husband, with your friend, with your wife, then it becomes very difficult.

Can you look at your wife, husband, neighbor, your politicians; can you look with eyes that have not this intervening space as created by the image? Can you look at yourself without condemning or justifying? The justification and condemnation is the censor. The censor is the conditioned entity. The conditioned entity is the 'me', the 'me' that says I must be more successful, the 'me' that says I must have more pleasure. So can you look at yourself without any distraction of thought? Are you following all of this? Have you done it?

Can you forget yourself, though you have identified yourself with something? That very identification is the continuance of the self. I identify myself with India. Myself has become the idea of India. And if you say anything against India, I get hurt; as long as you flatter it, I am pleased.

145

I identify myself with a belief, and I will fight to the death any attempt to destroy that identification because the moment I don't identify with something I am forced to look at myself. I don't want to look at myself because I am frightened to look at myself.[64]

*K*rishnamurti: One must be very clear, mustn't one, of the nature of desire; and desire is part of sensation, and thought identifies itself with that sensation, and through identification the 'I' is built up, the ego, and the ego then says, "I must," or "I will not."

So we are trying to find out if there is an action not based on the principle of ideals, on desire, on will; not spontaneous—that word is rather a dangerous word because nobody is spontaneous, one thinks one can be spontaneous, but there is no such thing because one must be totally free to be spontaneous. Do you follow?

So is there such action? Because most of our action has a motive. And motive means movement—I want to build a house, I want that woman, or that man, I am hurt psychologically or biologically and my motive is to hurt back—so there is always some kind of motive in action, which we do in daily life. So then action is conditioned by the motive. The motive is part of the identification process. So if I understand—not 'understand'—if there is a perception of the truth that identification builds the whole nature, the structure of the self, then is there an action which doesn't spring from thought? I don't know, am I right sir?

David Bohm: Could we ask why—before we go into that—why there is identification, why is it that this is so prevalent?

K: Why does thought identify.

DB: With sensation and other things.

K: Why is there identification with something? In identification there is duality, the identifier and the identified. When there is no identification, the senses are senses. But why does thought identify itself with senses?

DB: Yes, that is not yet clear.

K: We are going to make it clear.

DB: Are you saying that when the sensation is remembered, then we have identification?

K: Yes.

DB: Can we make that more clear?

K: Let's make it a little more clear. Let's work at it. There is perceiving a pleasurable lake, seeing a beautiful lake, what takes place in that seeing? There is not only optical seeing by the eye, but also the senses are awakened, the smell of the water, the trees on the lake—

DB: Could we stop a moment? When you say seeing, of course you see through the visual sense.

K: I am using purely visual sense.

DB: Therefore you already have the visual sense awakened merely to see. Is that what you mean?

K: Yes. Just seeing.

DB: Visually.

K: Visually, optically, I am just seeing, then what takes place?

DB: And the other senses start to operate.

K: And the other senses start operating. Why doesn't it stop there?

147

DB: What is the next step?

K: The next step is thought comes in—how beautiful that is, I wish I could remain here.

DB: So thought identifies it.

K: Yes.

DB: It says, "It is this."

K: Because in that there is pleasure.

DB: In what?

K: Seeing and the delight of seeing, then thought coming into operation and saying, "I must have more, I must build a house here, it is mine."

DB: But why does thought do that?

K: Why does thought interfere with senses—is that it? Now wait a minute, sir. The moment the senses take pleasure, say, "How delightful," and stop there, thought doesn't enter. Now why does thought enter? If it is painful, thought avoids it, it doesn't identify itself with that.

DB: It identifies against it, it says, "I don't want it."

K: No, leave it alone, go away from it, either deny it or move away from it. But if it is pleasurable, when the senses begin to enjoy, say, "How nice," then thought begins to identify itself with it.

DB: But why, I mean?

K: Why, because of pleasure.

148

DB: But why doesn't it give it up when it sees how futile this is?

K: Oh, that's much later.

DB: That's a long way on.

K: When it becomes painful, when it is aware identification breeds both pleasure and fear, then it begins to question.

DB: Well, are you saying that thought has made a simple mistake in the beginning, a kind of innocent mistake?

K: That's right. Thought has made a mistake in identifying with something that brings to it pleasure, or there is pleasure in something.

DB: And thought tries to take over.

K: To take over.

DB: To make it permanent, perhaps.

K: Permanent, that's right, which means memory. A remembrance of the lake with the daffodils and the trees and the water and sunlight, and all the rest of it.

DB: I understand thought has made a mistake and later it discovers that mistake, but it seems to be too late because it doesn't know how to stop.

K: It is now conditioned.

DB: So can we make it clear why it cannot give it up, you see.

K: Why it cannot give it up. That's our whole problem.

DB: Can we try to make it more clear.

K: Why doesn't thought give up something which it knows, or is aware is painful?

DB: Yes.

K: It is destructive. Why? Let's take a simple example: psychologically one is hurt.

DB: Well that is later.

K: I am taking that as an example, doesn't matter later. One is hurt; why can't one immediately give up that hurt, because knowing that hurt is going to create a great deal of damage? That is, when I am hurt I build a wall around myself not to be hurt more, there is fear, and isolation, neurotic actions, all that follows. Thought has created the image about myself, and that image gets hurt. Why doesn't thought say, "Yes, by Jove, I have seen this," drop it immediately? It is the same question. Because when it drops the image, there is nothing left.

DB: Then you have another ingredient because thought wants to hold on to the memory of the image.

K: Hold on to the memories which have created the image.

DB: And which may create it again, and thought feels they are very precious.

K: Yes, they are very precious, nostalgic, and all the rest of it.

DB: So somehow it gives very high value to all that. How did it come to do that?

K: Why has it made the image so valuable. Why has the image become so important which thought has created?

150

DB: If I may say that in the beginning it was a simple mistake, and thought made an image of pleasure and it seemed to become very important, precious, and was unable to give it up.

K: Yes, why doesn't it? Sir, if I give up pleasure, if thought gives up pleasure, what is there left?

DB: It can't seem to return to the state in the beginning when there was nothing.

K: Ah, that is the pristine state.

DB: It is unable to return to that state. Well, I think what happens is that when thought thinks of giving up pleasure which has become very precious, then the mere thought of that is painful.

K: Yes, giving up is painful.

DB: And therefore thought runs away from that.

K: Yes, so it clings to pleasure.

DB: It does not wish to face the pain.

K: Until there is a better reward for pleasure, which will be a better pleasure.

DB: That's no change.

K: Of course.

DB: But thought seems to have fallen into a trap which it has made because it has innocently remembered pleasure, and then gradually made it important; and then it has become too painful to give it up because any change from the immediate removal of pleasure is very painful.

151

K: Because it has nothing else then afterwards, then it is frightened. So it clings to something which it knows.

DB: Which it knows and which is very precious to it.

K: But it doesn't know that it is going to breed fear.

DB: Even when it knows, it still clings.

K: But it would much rather run away from fear, hoping the pleasure will continue.

DB: Eventually it starts to become irrational because it creates pressures which make the brain irrational and unable to get this straight.

K: Yes. We started off—didn't we?—with: is there an action in which there is no motive, no cause, the self doesn't enter into it at all? Of course there is. There is when the self is not, which means no identifying process takes place. There is the perceiving of a beautiful lake with all the color and the glory and the beauty of it, that's enough. Not the cultivating of memory, which is developed through the identification process.

DB: This raises the question: how are we going to stop this identification?

K: I don't think there is a 'how'. You see, that means meditation, control, practice, practice, practice. And that way makes the mind mechanical, dull—forgive me—and literally incapable of receiving anything new.

DB: I think that ordinarily we are identified with our language, and therefore it is driving us, but if we are free of identification—

K: That's right, sir, It is extraordinary how language has made us: "I am a communist."

DB: That's an identification.

K: That's it.

DB: But do you think that language is the major source of identification?

K: One of them.

DB: One of the big ones.

K: Yes.[65]

Questioner: What do you mean by 'identify'?

Krishnamurti: I love you, I have identified myself with you. Or, I have hurt her, and you identify yourself with her and get angry with me. See what has happened: I have said something to her which is harmful and unpleasant; you are her friend, you identify yourself with her and get angry with me. So that is part of the self-centered activity, isn't it? Are you sure?

I like you, I am very fond of you—what does that mean? I like your looks, you are a good companion, and so on. It means what?

Q: It means you are a better companion than other people and so I like being with you.

K: Go a little deeper. What does it mean?

Q: You keep that person to yourself and exclude others.

K: That is part of it, but go further.

Q: It is pleasing to be with that person.

K: It is pleasing to be with that person and it is not

pleasing with another person. So my relationship with you is based on my pleasure. If I don't like you I say, "I'll be off!" My pleasure is my concern, as is my hurt, my anger. So self-concern isn't just thinking about myself and identifying with this or that possession, person, or book. Is that what you do all day? There is the peripheral occupation, and also I am comparing myself with you; that is going on all the time, but from a center.

Q: You read about the refugees in India and you haven't a personal relationship with them but you do identify with them.

K: Why do I identify myself with those people who have been killed and chased out of East Pakistan? I watched them the other day on television; this is happening everywhere, not only in Pakistan, it is appalling. Now you say you identify yourself with all those refugees—what do you feel?

Q: Sympathy.

K: Go on, explore it, unravel it.

Q1: Anger against the people who caused this.

Q2: Frustration because you can't do anything about it.

K: You get angry with the people who do these things, who kill the young men and chase out old women and children. Is that what you do? You identify with this and reject that. What is the structure, the analysis of this identification?

Q: It is dualistic.

K: Move on.

Q: You don't feel secure.

K: Through identification you feel that you could do something?

Q: Even by taking one side you feel that you have a certain chance to do something.

K: I am anti-catholic; I identify myself with a group who are anti-clerical. Identifying myself with those, I feel I can do something. But go further, it is still me doing something about it, it is still the occupation with myself. I have identified myself with what I consider greater: India, communism, Catholicism, and so on. My family, my god, my belief, my house, you have hurt me—you follow? What is the reason for this identification?

Q: I separate myself from the rest of the world and in identifying with something bigger, that something becomes my ally.

K: Yes, but why do you do this? I identify myself with you because I like you. I don't identify myself with him because I don't like him. And I identify myself with my family, with my country, with my god, with my belief. Now why do I identify with anything at all—I don't say it is right or wrong—what is behind this identification?

Q: Inward confusion.

K: Is it?

Q: You are afraid.

K: Push further.

Q: The confusion is caused by the identification.

K: Is it? I am questioning you and you must question me too. Don't accept what I am saying, inquire. This whole process of identification, why does it happen? And if I don't identify myself with you, or with something, I feel frustrated. Are you sure?

Q1: I don't know.

Q2: You feel unfulfilled, empty.

K: Go on. I feel sad, frustrated, not fulfilled, insufficient, empty. Now I want to know why I identify myself with a group, with a community, with feelings, ideas, ideals, heroes, and all the rest of it—why?

Q: I think it is in order to have security.

K: Yes. But what do you mean by that word *security?*

Q: Alone I am weak.

K: Is it because you cannot stand alone?

Q: It is because you are afraid to stand alone.

K: You are frightened of being alone, so therefore you identify?

Q: Not always.

K: But it is the core, the root of it. Why do I want to identify myself? Because then I feel safe. I have pleasant memories of people and places so, I identify myself with that. I see in identification I am much more secure, right?

Q: I don't know if you want to talk about this particular aspect, but if I see the killing in Vietnam is wrong, and there is a group of anti-war demonstrators in Washington, then I go and join them.

156

K: Now wait a minute. There is an antiwar group and I join them. I identify myself with them because in identifying with a group of people who are doing something about it, I am also doing something about it; by myself I cannot do anything. But belonging to a group of people who demonstrate, who write articles and say, "It is terrible," I am actively taking part in stopping the war. That is the identification. We are not seeking the results of that identification—whether it is good or bad. But why does the human mind want to identify itself with something?

The identification takes place because you feel, "Here I am secure." So is the reason you identify because you are insecure? Is that it? Insecurity means fear, uncertainty, not to know what to think, to be confused. So you need protection—it is good to have protection. Is that the reason why you identify?

What is the next step? In myself I am uncertain, unclear, confused, frightened, and insufficient; therefore, I identify myself with a belief. Now what happens?

Q: I find I am still insecure.

K: No. I have identified myself with certain ideologies. What happens then?

Q: You try to make that your security.

K: I have given various reasons for this identification: because it is rational, it is workable, all the rest of it. Now what happens when I have identified myself with it?

Q: You have a conflict.

K: Look what happens. I have identified myself—with an ideology, with a group of people, or a person, it is part of me. I must protect that, mustn't I? Therefore, if it is threatened I am lost, I am back again to my insecurity. So what takes place? I am angry with anybody who attacks or doubts it. Then what is the actual thing that takes place?

Q: Conflict.

K: Look: I have identified myself with an ideology. I must protect it because it is my security and I resist anybody who threatens that, in the sense of having a contradictory ideology. So where I have identified myself with an ideology, there must be resistance; I build a wall round what I have identified myself with. Where there is a wall, it must create division. Then there is conflict. I don't know if you see all this?

Now what is the next step?—go on.

Q1: What is the difference between identification and cooperation?

Q2: It seems there has to be more understanding of cooperation.

K: You know what it means to cooperate, to work together? Can there be cooperation when there is identification? Do you know what we mean by identification? We have examined the anatomy of it. Cooperation means to work together. Can I work with you if I have identified myself with an ideology, and you are identified with another ideology? Obviously not.

Q: But people have to work together.

K: Is that cooperation?

Q: No.

K: See what is involved. Because of our identification with an ideology, we work together; you protect it and I protect it. It is our security, in the name of God, in the name of beauty, in the name of anything. We think that is

158

cooperation. Now what takes place? Can there be cooperation when there is identification with a group?

Q: No, because there is division. I find myself in conflict
with members of the group because I keep identifying with
them.

K: Look what is happening. You and I have identified
ourselves with that ideology. Our interpretation of that ideology may be—

Q: . . . different . . .

K: Of course. If you vary in the interpretation of that
ideology you are deviating, therefore we are in conflict.
Therefore we must both of us agree about that ideology
completely. Is that possible?

Q: That is exactly what happens with a school. Instead of
an ideology, you identify with a school, and each person has
his own concept.

K: Yes, quite right—why?

Q: I sense that sometimes there is conflict here for just
the reason you were giving when talking about an ideology.
If you and I identify with the school, we think we are coop-
erating, but there isn't that spirit.

K: Therefore I am asking, can there be cooperation when
there is identification?

Q: No.

K: Do you know what you are saying? [*Laughter.*]
That is how everything in this world is working. Is that the
truth—that where there is identification, there can be no
cooperation? It is a marvelous thing to discover the truth of
this. Not your opinion, or my opinion, but the truth, the

159

validity of it. Therefore, we have to find out what we mean by cooperation. You see, there can be no cooperation when there is identification with an idea, with a leader, with a group, and so on. Then, what is cooperation in which there is no identification?

Q: Acting in response to the situation itself.

K: I am not saying you are not right, but can we work together when you and I think differently? When you are concerned with yourself and I am concerned with myself? And one of the reasons is that knowing we cannot cooperate when we are thinking of ourselves, we try to identify ourselves with an ideology, hoping thereby to bring about cooperation. But if you don't identify, what is cooperation?

Here we are at Brockwood, in a school. We see there cannot be cooperation when there is identification with the school, with an idea, with a program, with a particular policy of this and that. And also we see that identification is the cause of all division. Then, what is cooperation? To work together, not "about something." Do you see the difference? So before you do something together, what is the spirit of cooperation? The feeling, the inwardness of it, what is that feeling?

Q: Understanding, being completely open to it.

K: Go a little deeper. We said identification is not cooperation. Are you quite sure on that point? And are you quite clear that cooperation cannot exist when each of us is concerned with himself? But you are concerned with yourself, therefore you have no spirit of cooperation, you only cooperate when it pleases you. So what does it mean to cooperate? We are not playing parlor games. What does it mean to cooperate when there is no 'me'?—otherwise you can't cooperate. I may try to cooperate round an idea, but there is always the 'me'.[66]

160

Questioner: You say that through identification we bring about separation, division. Your way of life appears to some of us to be separative and isolating and to have caused division among those who were formerly together. With what have you identified yourself?

Krishnamurti: Now, let us first see the truth of the statement that identification divides, separates. I have stated that several times. Is it a fact or not?

What do we mean by identification? Don't just merely and verbally indulge in it, but look at it directly. You identify yourself with your country. Don't you? When you do that, what happens? You immediately enclose yourself through that identification with a particular group. That is a fact, is it not?

When you call yourself a Hindu, you have identified yourself with particular beliefs, traditions, hopes, ideas; and that very identification isolates you. That is a fact, is it not?

If you see the truth of that, then you cease to identify; therefore, you are no longer a Hindu or a Buddhist or a Christian, politically or religiously. So, identification is separative, is a deteriorating factor in life. That is a fact; that is the truth of it, whether you like it or not.

The questioner goes on to ask if I have, through my action, brought about division among those who were formerly together. Quite right. If you see something true, must you not state it? Though it brings trouble, though it brings about disunity, should you not state it? How can there be unity on falsity? You identify yourself with a idea, with a belief, and when another questions that belief, the idea, you throw that other fellow out. You don't bring him in, you push him out. You have isolated him; the man who says what you are doing is wrong has not isolated you. So, your action is isolating, and not his action, not the action of the person who points to the truth. You don't want to face the fact that identification is separative.

Identification with a family, with an idea, with a belief, with any particular organization is all separative. When that is directly put an end to, or when you are made to look at it and are given a challenge, then you who want to identify, who want to be separative, who want to push the other fellow out, say that man is isolating.

Your way of existence, your way of life, is separative; and so you are responsible for separation, I am not. You have thrown me out; I have not gone out. Naturally, you begin to feel that I am isolating, that I am bringing division, that my ideas and my expressions are destroying, are destructive. They should be destructive; they should be revolutionary. Otherwise, what is the value of anything new?

Surely, sirs, there must be revolution, not according to any particular ideology or pattern. If it is according to an ideology or pattern, then it is not revolution, it is merely the continuation of the past; it is identification with a new idea and therefore it gives continuity to a particular form; and that is certainly not revolution.

Revolution comes into being when there is an inward cessation of all identification; and you can only do that, when you are capable of looking straight at the fact without deceiving yourself and without giving the interpreter a chance to tell you what he thinks of it.

Seeing the truth of identification, obviously I am not identified with anything. When I see a truth that something hurts, there is no problem; I leave it alone. I cease to identify there or elsewhere. You realize that the whole process of identification is destructive, separative; whether this process takes place in religious beliefs or in the political dialectical outlook, it is all separative. When you recognize that, when you see that and are fully aware of it, then obviously you are freed; therefore there is no identification with anything. Not to be identified means to stand alone, but not as a noble entity facing the world. This has nothing to do with being together. But, you are afraid of disunity.

The questioner says I have brought disunity. Have I? I doubt it! You have discovered for yourself the truth of it. If you are persuaded by me and therefore identify yourself with me, then you have not done a new thing; you have only exchanged one evil for another.

We must break to find out. The real revolution is the inward revolution; it is a revolution that sees things clearly and that is of love. In that state, you have no identification with anything.[67]

AWARENESS IS A PROCESS OF DISCOVERY, which becomes blocked through identification. When we are rightly aware of greed in its complexity, there is no struggle against it, no negative assertion of nongreed, which is only another form of self-assertiveness; and in that awareness we will find that greed has ceased.

Our difficulty lies in that we have built around ourselves conclusions which we call 'understanding.' These conclusions are hindrances to understanding. If you go into this more deeply, you will see that there must be complete abandonment of all that has been accumulated for the being of understanding and wisdom. To be simple is not a conclusion, an intellectual concept for which you strive. There can be simplicity only when the self with its accumulation ceases.

It is comparatively easy to renounce family, property, fame, things of the world; that is only a beginning; but it is extremely difficult to put away all knowledge, all conditioned memory. In this freedom, this aloneness, there is experience which is beyond and above all creations of the mind. Do not let us ask whether the mind ever can be free from conditioning, from influence; we shall find this out as we proceed in self-knowledge and understanding. Thought, which is a result, cannot understand the causeless.

The ways of accumulation are subtle; accumulation is self-assertiveness, as is imitation. To come to a conclusion is to build a wall around oneself, a protective security which prevents understanding. Accumulated conclusions do not make for wisdom but only sustain the self. Without accumulation there is no self. A mind weighed down with accumulations is incapable of following the swift movement of life, incapable of deep and pliable awareness.

Questioner: Being imitative what shall we do?

163

Krishnamurti: Be self-aware, which will reveal the hidden motives of imitation, envy, fear, the craving for security, for power, and so on. This awareness, when free of self-identification, brings understanding and tranquillity which lead to the realization of supreme wisdom.

Q: Is not this process of awareness, of self-unfoldment, another form of acquisition? Is not probing another means of self-expansive acquisitiveness?

K: If the questioner experimented with awareness, he would discover the truth about his question. Understanding is never accumulative; understanding comes only when there is stillness, when there is passive alertness. There is no stillness, no passivity when the mind is acquisitive; acquisitiveness is ever restless, envious. As we said, awareness is not cumulative; through identification, accumulation is built up, giving continuity to the self through memory.

To be aware without self-identification, without condemnation or justification is extremely arduous, for our response is based on pleasure and pain, reward and punishment. How few are aware of constant identification; if we were we would not ask these questions which indicate unawareness. As a sleeper dreams that he must awaken but does not, for it is only a dream, so we are asking these questions without actually experimenting with awareness.

Q: Is there anything that one can do to be aware?

K: Are you not in conflict, in sorrow? If you are, do you not search out its cause? The cause is the self, its torturing desires. To struggle with these desires only creates resistance, further pain, but if you are choicelessly aware of your craving, then there comes creative understanding. It is the truth of this understanding that liberates, not your struggle against resistance to envy, anger, pride, and so on.

So awareness is not an act of will, for will is resistance, the effort made by the self through desire to acquire, to grow,

164

whether positively or negatively. Be aware of acquisitiveness, passively observing its ways on different levels; you will find this rather arduous, for thought-feeling sustains itself on identification, and it is this which prevents the understanding of accumulation.

Be aware, take the journey of self-discovery. Do not ask what is going to happen on this journey, which only betrays anxiety, fear, indicating your desire for security, for certainty. This desire for refuge prevents self-knowledge, self-unfoldment and so, understanding. Be aware of this inward anxiety and directly experience it; then you will discover what this awareness reveals. But unfortunately most of you only desire to talk about the journey without undertaking it.

Q: What happens to us at the end of the journey?

K: Is it not important for the questioner to be aware of why he is asking this question? Is it not because of the fear of the unknown, the desire to gain an end, or the assurance of self-continuity? Being in sorrow we seek happiness; being impermanent we search after the permanent; being in darkness we look for light. But if we were aware of *what is*, then the truth of sorrow, of impermanence, of imprisonment would liberate thought from its own ignorance.

Q: Is there no such thing as creative thinking?

K: It would be rather vain to consider what is creativeness. If we were aware of our conditioning, then the truth of this would bring about creative being. To speculate upon creative being is a hindrance; all speculation is a hindrance to understanding. Only when the mind is simple, purged of all self-deception and cunning, cleansed of all accumulation, is there the real. The purgation of the mind is not an act of will nor the outcome of imitative compulsion. Awareness of *what is*, is liberating.[68]

165

*A*WARENESS IS THE SOLUTION OF OUR PROBLEMS; we must experiment with it and discover its truth. It would be folly merely to accept; to accept is not to understand. Acceptance or nonacceptance is a positive act which hinders experimentation and understanding. Understanding that comes through experiment and self-knowledge brings confidence.

This confidence may be called faith. It is not the faith of the foolish; it is not faith in something. Ignorance may have faith in wisdom, darkness in light, cruelty in love, but such faith is still ignorance. This confidence or faith of which I am speaking comes through experimentation in self-knowledge, not through acceptance and hope.

The self-confidence that many have is the outcome of ignorance, of achievement, of self-glory, or of capacity. The confidence of which I speak is understanding, not the "I understand," but understanding without self-identification. The confidence or faith in something, however noble, breeds only obstinacy, and obstinacy is another term for credulity.

The clever ones have destroyed blind faith, but when they themselves are in serious conflict or sorrow, they accept faith or become cynical. To believe is not to be religious; to have faith in something which is created by the mind is not to be open to the real.

Confidence comes into being, it cannot be manufactured by the mind; confidence comes with experiment and discovery; not the experiment with belief, theory, or memory but experimentation with self-knowledge. This confidence or faith is not self-imposed nor is it identified with belief, formulation, hope. It is not the outcome of self-expanding desire. In experimenting with awareness there is a discovery which is freeing in its understanding. This self-knowledge through passive awareness is from moment to moment, without accumulation; it is endless, truly creative. Through awareness there comes vulnerability to truth.

To be open, vulnerable to the real, thought must cease to be accumulative. It is not that thought-feeling must *become* nongreedy, which is still accumulative, a negative form of self-expansion, but it must *be* nongreedy. A greedy mind is a conflicting mind; a greedy mind is ever fearful, envious in its self-growth and fulfillment. Such a mind is ever changing the objects of its desire, and this changing is considered growth; a greedy mind which renounces the world in order to seek reality, God, is still greedy; greed is ever restless, ever seeking growth, fulfillment, and this restless activity creates self-assertive intelligence but is not capable of understanding the real.

Greed is a complex problem! To live in the world of greed without greed needs deep understanding; to live simply, earning a right livelihood in a world organized on economic aggression and expansion is possible only for those who are discovering inward riches.

Questioner: Is there a technique for being aware?

Krishnamurti: What does this question imply? You seek a method by which you may learn to be aware. Awareness is not the result of practice, habit, or time. As a tooth that causes intense pain has to be attended to immediately, so sorrow, if intense, demands urgent alleviation. But instead we seek an escape or explain it away; we avoid the real issue which is the self.

Because we are not facing our conflict, our sorrow, we assure ourselves lazily that we must make an effort to be aware, and so we demand a technique for becoming aware.[69]

THE OBSERVER AND THE OBSERVED ARE ONE; the thinker and his thoughts are one. To experience the thinker and his thought as one is very arduous, for the thinker is ever taking shelter behind his thought; he separates himself from his thoughts to safeguard himself, to give himself continuity, permanency; he modifies or changes his thoughts, but he remains. This pursuit of thought apart from himself, this changing, transforming it, leads to illusion. The thinker is his thought; the thinker and his thoughts are not two separate processes.

We generally regard our thoughts as being apart from ourselves; we are not aware of the thinker and his thought as

167

one. This is precisely the difficulty. After all, the qualities of the self are not separate from the self; the self is not something apart from its thoughts, from its attributes. The self is put together, made up, and the self is not, when the parts are dissolved.

But, in illusion, the self separates itself from its qualities in order to protect itself, to give itself continuity, permanency. It takes refuge in its qualities through separating itself from them. The self asserts that it is this and it is that; the self, the I, modifies, changes, transforms its thoughts, its qualities, but this change only gives strength to the self, to its protective walls. But if you are aware deeply, you will perceive that the thinker and his thoughts are one; the observer is the observed.

To experience this actual integrated fact is extremely difficult, and right meditation is the way to this integration.

The additive process prevents the experiencing of the real. Where there is accumulation there is a becoming of the self, which is the cause of conflict and pain. The accumulative desire for pleasure and the avoidance of pain is a becoming. Awareness is nonaccumulative for it is ever discovering truth, and truth can only be when there is no accumulation, when there is no imitation.[70]

*A*WARENESS IS OBSERVATION without condemnation. Awareness brings understanding because there is no condemnation or identification, but silent observation. Surely, if I want to understand something, I must observe, I must not criticize, I must not condemn, I must not pursue it as pleasure or avoid it as nonpleasure. There must merely be the silent observation of a fact. There is no end in view, but awareness of everything as it arises. That observation and the understanding of that observation cease when there is condemnation, identification, or justification.

Awareness is not self-improvement. On the contrary, it is the ending of the self, of the 'I', with all its peculiar idiosyncrasies, memories, demands, and pursuits. In awareness, there is no condemnation or identification; therefore, there is no self-improvement. There is a vast difference between the two. The man who wants to improve himself can never be aware, because improvement implies condemnation and the achievement of a result. Whereas, in awareness, there is observation without condemnation, without denial or acceptance.

That awareness begins with outward things, being aware, being in contact with objects, with nature. First, there is awareness of things about one, being sensitive to objects, to nature, then to people, which means relationship, and then there is awareness of ideas. This awareness, being sensitive to things, to nature, to people, to ideas, is not made up of separate processes, but is one unitary process. It is a constant observation of everything, of every thought and feeling and action as they arise within oneself. And as awareness is not condemnatory, there is no accumulation. You condemn only when you have a standard, which means there is accumulation, and therefore improvement of the self.

Awareness is to understand the activities of the self, the 'I', in its relationship with people, with ideas, and with things. That awareness is from moment to moment, and therefore it cannot be practiced. When you practice a thing, it becomes a habit; and awareness is not habit. A mind that is habitual is insensitive; a mind that is functioning within the groove of a particular action is dull, unpliable; whereas, awareness demands constant pliability, alertness.

This is not difficult. It is what you all do when you are interested in something, when you are interested in watching your child, your wife, your plants, trees, birds. You observe without condemnation, without identification; therefore, in that observation, there is complete communion, the observer and the observed are completely in communion. This actually takes place when you are deeply, profoundly interested in something.

Awareness is a process of release from the action of the self; it is to be aware of your daily movements, of your thoughts, of your actions, and to be aware of another, to observe him. You can do that only when you love somebody, when you are deeply interested in something; and when I want to know myself, my whole being, the whole content of myself and not just one or two layers, then there obviously must be no condemnation. Then I must be open to every thought, to every feeling, to all the moods, to all the suppressions; and as there is more and more expansive awareness, there is greater and greater freedom from all the hidden movement of thoughts, motives, and pursuits. So, awareness is freedom, it brings freedom, it yields freedom.

Now, when you have a profound experience of any kind, what is taking place? When there is such an experience, are you aware that you are experiencing? When you are angry, at the split second of anger or of jealousy or of joy, are you aware that you are joyous or that you are angry? It is only when the experience is over that there is the experiencer and the experienced. Then the experiencer observes the experienced, the object of experience. But at the moment of experience, there is neither the observer nor the observed: there is only the experiencing.

Now, most of us are not experiencing. We are always outside the state of experiencing, and therefore we ask this question as to who is the observer, who is it that is aware. Surely, such a question is a wrong question, is it not? The moment there is experiencing, there is neither the person who is aware nor the object of which he is aware. There is neither the observer nor the observed, but only a state of experiencing.

Most of us find it is extremely difficult to live in a state of experiencing, because that demands an extraordinary pliability, a quickness, a high degree of sensitivity; and that is denied when we are pursuing a result, when we want to succeed, when we have an end in view, when we are calculating—all of which brings frustration. But a man who does not demand anything, who is not seeking an end, who is not searching out a result with all its implications, such a man is in a state of constant experiencing. Everything then has a movement, a meaning, and nothing is old; nothing is charred, nothing is repetitive, because *what is*, is never old.

The challenge is always new. It is only the response to the challenge that is old; and the old creates further residue, which is memory, the observer, who separates himself from the observed, from the challenge, from the experience. You can experiment with this for yourself very simply and very easily. Next time you are angry or jealous or greedy or violent or whatever it be, watch yourself. In that state, 'you' are not. There is only that state of being. But the moment, the second afterwards, you term it, you name it, you call it jealousy, anger, greed. So, you have created immediately the observer and the observed, the experiencer and the experienced.

When there is the experiencer and the experienced, then the experiencer tries to modify the experience, change it, remember things about it, and so on, and therefore maintains the division between himself and the experienced.

But if you don't name that feeling—which means you are not seeking a result, you are not condemning, you are merely silently aware of the feeling—then you will see that in that state of feeling, of experiencing, there is no observer and no observed; because the observer and the observed are a joint phenomenon, and there is only experiencing. Awareness is a state in which there is no condemnation, no justification or identification, and therefore there is understanding; and in that state of passive, alert awareness, there is neither the experiencer nor the experienced.

Sir, what I am saying is not very difficult, though you may find it verbally difficult. But you will notice, when you yourself are interested in something very gravely and very deeply, this actually takes place. You are so completely submerged in the thing in which you are interested that there is no exclusion, no concentration.

Awareness is a state in which truth can come into being, the truth of *what is*, the simple truth of daily existence. It is only when we understand the truth of daily existence that we can go far. You must begin near to go far; but most of us want to jump, to begin far without understanding what is close. As we understand the near, we will find the distance between the near and the far is not. There is no distance—the beginning and the end are one.[71]

Questioner: I have listened to what you have been saying and I feel that to carry out your teachings, I must renounce the world I live in.

Krishnamurti: Sir, you cannot renounce the world, can you? What is the world? The world is made up of things, relationships, and ideas. How can you give up things? Even if you give up your house, you will still have a 'kurtha' [clothing].

You may renounce your wife but you will still be in relation with someone, with the milkman, for instance, or the man who gives you food. And you cannot renounce belief, can you? I wish you would. Begin there, if you must renounce something, renounce the wrong valuations which you have given to everything. Wrong valuations create havoc, and it is from these wrong valuations, which cause misery, that you want to escape.

You don't want to understand that you are giving wrong values. You want to escape from the result of wrong values but if you understood the world—which is ideas, relationship, things, and their true significance—then you would not be in conflict with the world. You cannot withdraw from the world, to withdraw means isolation and you cannot live in isolation. You can live in isolation only in an asylum, but not by renouncing the world.

You can only live truly happily with the world when you are not of the world, which means you don't give wrong values to the things in the world. This can happen only when you understand yourself, the giver of wrong values.

It is like a stupid man trying to renounce stupidity. He will still be stupid; he may try to become clever, but he will remain stupid. But if he understood what stupidity is—that is, himself—surely then he would reach great heights. Then he would have wisdom. It is not by renouncing that you can find reality. By renouncing you escape into illusion; you do not discover that which is true.

So, what I have been saying is that one must give right values to things, to relationship, to ideas and not try to escape from the world. It is comparatively easy to go away into isolation, but it is extremely arduous to be aware and to give true values.

Things have no value in themselves. The house has no value in itself, but it has the value you give it. If psychologically you are empty, insufficient in yourself, the house becomes very important because you identify yourself with the house, and then comes the problem of attachment and renunciation. It is really stupid, and if you understood your inward nature, your inward hollowness, then the problem would have very little meaning.

Everything becomes extraordinarily significant when you are trying to use it to cover up your own loneliness. Similarly with relationship, with ideas, with belief. So, there is richness only in understanding the significance of *what is*, and not in running away into isolation.

It does not matter what any book says. Is the thinker separate from his thought? If he is separate, problems will continue; if he is not, then he can be freed of the source of all problems.

If the thinker is separate from his thoughts, how does he become separated? Remove the qualities of the thinker, remove his thoughts, where is the thinker? The thinker is not. Remove the qualities of the self, which is memory, ambition, and so on, where is the self? But if you say the self is not the thinker but some other entity behind the thinker, he is still the thinker, because you have only pushed the thinker further back.

Now, why has the thinker separated himself from his thoughts? The thinker cannot be without thought because if there is no thought there is no thinker.

Now the thinker has separated himself from the thought for the simple reason that thought can be transformed, can be modified, and so in order to give himself permanency the thinker separates himself from the thought and thereby gives himself permanency.

The thought being transient, mutable, can be altered, but the thinker who creates the thought can be permanent. He is the permanent entity, whereas the thought is changeable, it can be changed according to circumstances, according to environmental influences, but he the thinker remains. He is the thought and if thought ceases, he is not, surely, although all our books say differently.

Just think it out for yourself for the first time. Put your books aside, forget your authorities, and look at the problem directly. Without the thought the thinker is not, and the thinker creates the thought and separates himself from it in order to protect himself; thereby he gives stability, certainty to himself, and continuity.

Now, how does the thinker come into being? Obviously through desire. Desire is the outcome of perception, contact, sensation, identification, and 'me'. Perception of a car, contact, sensation, desire, identification, and "I like it," "I want it." So, I am the product, the thinker is the product of desire, and having produced the 'I', the 'I' separates itself from the thought, because it can then transform the thought and yet remain permanent.

So, as long as the thinker is separate from his thought, there will be problems, one after the other, innumerable problems; but if there is no separation, if the thinker is the thought, then what happens? Then the thinker himself undergoes a transformation, a radical, fundamental transformation, and that, as I have said, is meditation.

It is self-knowledge, it is all that I have said about the thinker; how he separates himself from the thought and how the thinker has come into being. You can test it for yourself. You don't have to read a sacred book to find out the truth of it. That is the beginning of self-knowledge, and from that there comes meditation.

Meditation is the ending of thought, of the thinker, by not giving significance to the thinker, by not giving continuity to the thinker. The thinker is disciplining his thought, separating himself so as to give continuity to himself through property, through family, through ideas, and as long as the thinker exists there will be problems, and it is when the thinker ceases thinking, that meditation begins.

Meditation is self-knowledge and without self-knowledge there is no meditation. You will find that if you go into the whole question of self-knowledge, which is the beginning of wisdom—not by any practice, because practice is merely resistance—you can go deeper and deeper, starting with the center, which is the desire creating the 'I', the self; and when that self continues in the Atman or higher self, it is still the thinker merely pushing further back his permanency.

Till you are aware of this whole process, there is no ending of the problem. But when you become aware, you will find that time has ceased—time as memory of the past and the future—and that there is the immediate present, the eternal, and in this alone is reality.[72]

IN THE VARIOUS TALKS THE SPEAKER HAS GIVEN, he has used the word *insight*. That is, to see into things, into the whole movement of thought, into the whole movement, for example, of jealousy, to perceive the nature of greed, to see the whole content of sorrow. It is not analysis, not exercise of intellectual capacity, nor is it the result of knowledge— knowledge being that which has been accumulated through the past as experience, stored up in the brain. Knowledge always goes with ignorance; there is no complete knowledge, therefore there is always knowledge and ignorance, like two horses tethered.

So then what is insight? If observation is not based on knowledge, or on intellectual capacity of reasoning, exploring, analyzing, then what is it? That is the whole question.

Is it intuition? That word *intuition* is rather a tricky word. The actuality of intuition may be the result of desire. One may desire something and then a few days later you have an intuition about it. And you think that intuition is most extraordinarily important. But if you go into it rather deeply, you may find that it is based on desire, on fear, on various forms of pleasure. So one is rather doubtful about that word, especially as it is used by those people who are rather romantic, who are rather imaginative, sentimental, and wanting something. They would certainly have intuitions, but these may be based on some obvious self-deceptive desire. So for the moment we can put aside that word *intuition*. I hope I am not hurting anybody who is caught in intuitions.

And if that is not so, then what is insight? That is, to perceive something instantly which must be true, logical, sane, rational. You understand? And that insight must act instantly. It isn't that I have an insight and do nothing about it.

I will explain a little bit about thinking. Thinking is the response of memory. Memory is the residue of experience, knowledge, stored up in the brain. And the memory responds. "Where do you live?" You answer. "What is your name?" There is immediate response. And so on.

Thought is the result or the response of accumulated experience, knowledge as memory. That is simple. Thought based upon knowledge is limited because knowledge is limited. So thought can never be all-inclusive. It must always be partial, limited, based on knowledge and ignorance. Therefore it is everlastingly confined, narrow. Now to have an insight into that means an action that is not merely the repetition of thought. To have an insight means that you are observing without memory, remembrances, without argumentation pro and con, just seeing the whole movement. And from that insight you act. And that action is logical, is sane, healthy. It is not that you have an insight, and then you do the opposite; then it is not insight. I wonder if you are getting all this? Sorry to be so emphatic. That is my way of doing it.

To have an insight, for example, into the wounds, hurts that one has received from childhood. We are all people who are hurt for various reasons; from childhood until we die, there is this wound in us, psychologically. Can you have an insight into the whole nature and structure of that hurt? Do you understand? Aren't you hurt, wounded psychologically? Play the game with me. The ball is in your court.

You are obviously hurt. You may go to a psychologist, analyst, psychotherapist, and they trace why you are hurt— from childhood your mother was this, and your father was that, and so on, and so on. But merely seeking out the cause is not going to resolve the hurt. It is there. And the consequences of that are isolation, fear, resistance, and the self-enclosure of not wanting to be hurt any more.

You know all this. That's the whole movement of being hurt. The hurt is the image that you have created for yourself about yourself. Right? So long as that image remains, you will be hurt. Obviously. When there is an insight into all that—without analysis, seeing it instantly—by the very perception of that insight, which demands all your attention and energy, the hurt is dissolved. And therefore when it is dissolved, there is no further hurt.

If one may ask most politely: you have heard this; have you got that insight that will dissolve your hurt completely, leaving no mark, and therefore no hurt, so that nobody can hurt you? Because the image that you have created about yourself is nonexistent. Are you following all this? Are you doing it? Or are you just merely verbally paying attention to the words?

Questioner: I don't really understand what you mean when you say we have created this hurt.

Krishnamurti: First of all, who is hurt? What do you mean by being hurt? Sir, what do you mean by being hurt? You say, "I am hurt"—consciously you are aware of it or not. One is hurt. Now what is that which is being hurt? Do you understand my question? What is that which is hurt? You say, "It is me." What is that 'me'? It is the image you have about yourself. If I have an image about myself: I am marvelous, spiritual, blah, blah, and you come along and say, "No, you are a silly ass"—I get hurt. That is, thought has created an image about oneself, and that image is always comparing. So as long as one has this image about oneself it is going to be trodden on by somebody, and that causes hurt, wounds, psychologically.

To have an insight into that means to see the whole movement, the cause and the image, and therefore the very perception ends the image.[73]

177

*W*HEN A MACHINE IS REVOLVING VERY FAST, as a fan with several blades, the separate parts are not visible but appear as one. So the self, the 'me', seems to be a unified entity, but if its activities can be slowed down, then we shall perceive that it is not a unified entity but made up of many separate and contending desires and pursuits. These separate wants and hopes, fears and joys make up the self.

The self is a term to cover craving in its different forms. To understand the self there must be an awareness of craving in its multiple aspects. The passive awareness, the choiceless discernment reveals the ways of the self, bringing freedom from bondage. Thus, when the mind is tranquil and free of its own activity and chatter, there is supreme wisdom.

Our problem then is how to free thought from its accumulated experiences, memories. How can this self cease to be? Deep and true experience takes place only when the activity of this accumulation ceases. We see that unless there is an experience of truth, none of our problems can be solved—whether sociological, religious, or personal. Conflict cannot come to an end by merely rearranging frontiers or reorganizing economic values or imposing a new ideology; throughout the centuries we have tried these many ways, but conflict and sorrow have continued.

Until there is a comprehension of the real, merely pruning the branches of our self-expansive activity is of little use, for the central problem remains unsolved. Until we discover truth there is no way out of our sorrows and problems. The solution is the direct experience of truth when the mind is still, in the tranquillity of awareness, in the openness of receptivity.

We often have religious experiences, sometimes vague, sometimes definite; experiences of intense devotion or joy, of being deeply vulnerable, of fleeting unity with all things; we try to utilize these experiences in meeting our difficulties and sorrows. These experiences are numerous, but our thought, caught in time, turmoil, and pain, tries to use them as stimulants to overcome our conflicts. We say God or truth will help us in our difficulties, but these experiences do not actually resolve our sorrow and confusion.

Such moments of deep experience come when thought is not active in its self-protective memories; these experiences are independent of our striving, and when we try to use them as stimulants for strength in our struggles, they only further the expansion of the self and its peculiar intelligence.

So we come back to our question: how can this intelligence of the self, so sedulously cultivated, cease? It can cease only through passive awareness.

Awareness is from moment to moment; it is not the cumulative effect of self-protective memories. Awareness is not determination, nor is it the action of will. Awareness is without rationalization, without the division of the observer and the observed. As awareness is nonaccumulative, non-residual, it does not build up the self, positively or negatively. Awareness is ever in the present and so, nonidentifying and nonrepetitive; nor does it create habit.

Take, for instance, the habit of smoking and experiment with it in awareness. Be aware of smoking, do not condemn, rationalize, or accept, simply be aware. If you are so aware there is the cessation of the habit; if you are so aware there will be no recurrence of it, but if you are not aware the habit will persist. This awareness is not the determination to cease or to indulge.

Be aware; there is a fundamental difference between being and becoming. To become aware you make effort, and effort implies resistance and time and leads to conflict. If you are aware in the moment there is no effort, no continuance of the self-protective intelligence. You are aware or you are not; the desire to be aware is only the activity of the sleeper, the dreamer.

Awareness reveals the problem completely, fully, without denial or acceptance, justification or identification, and it is freedom which quickens understanding. Awareness is a unitary process of the observer and the observed.

It is the petty mind that creates problems for itself, and through awareness of the cause of problems, the self, they are dissolved. To be aware of narrowness and its many results implies deep understanding of it on all the different levels of consciousness: pettiness in things, in relationship, in ideas.

When we are conscious of being petty or violent or envious, we make an effort not to be; we condemn it, for we desire to be something else. This condemnatory attitude puts an end to the understanding of *what is* and its process. The desire to put an end to greed is another form of self-assertion and so is the cause of continued conflict and pain.

Through awareness only can there be cessation of the cause of conflict. Be aware of any habit of thought or action; then you will recognize the rationalizing, condemnatory process which is preventing understanding. Through awareness—the reading of the book of habit page by page—comes self-knowledge.

It is truth that frees, not your effort to be free.[74]

Freedom

FREEDOM

*F*REEDOM IMPLIES, does it not, that you must not follow anyone? You must be free to inquire, not accept, not look to a guide, to a system, to a savior, to a guru. Freedom implies that you must have the capacity to inquire, not into what others say but to inquire within yourself, to investigate, to examine the whole structure of a human mind—that is, our mind, your mind.

Any form of conformity, imitation according to a pattern, a mold, does not allow free inquiry. And what we are going to talk about demands that you be free to listen—not only to the word but to the meaning of the word, and not be a slave to the word, not accept whatever the speaker says, or deny what he says, but listen to find out. To find out for yourself not according to some interpretation, not according to some other speaker, but to find out for yourself the truth or the falseness of what is being said.

Freedom is not to do what you want to do. That is not freedom at all. And I think probably *that* freedom has brought about great misery in the world—each one doing exactly what he wants to do. That is rampant in this country, where there is no tradition, where there is no discipline—I am using the word *discipline* in a totally different sense, which we will go into presently.

Freedom does not imply choice. One thinks one is free if you can choose. I do not know if you have ever gone into this question of choice. You have a vast array in front of you—the various teachers, yogis, philosophers, scientists, psychologists, analysts—bombarding your mind, constantly, day in and day out. And from this array you are going to choose whom you think you should follow, whom you think you should listen to.

You choose according to your temperament, according to your desire, according to your pleasure. Please do listen to this—if you will—carefully, because you are confronted with this problem, when so many of them are telling you: "Follow this and don't follow that" and "Do this" and "Do that." And you are faced with the question of whom to listen to and whom to follow, whether that teacher, that philosophy, that guru.

You are not free, and it is absolutely necessary to be free to find out what is true and what is false for yourself—which no one can tell you, no system, no philosophy, no guru. When you face this array of teachers, philosophers, and systems you are forced—because you yourself are confused, life has become terrible, painful, uncertain; there is so much poverty, the threat of destruction, violence, and you want to escape from all that—you are forced to choose one of these. And your choice is based upon your confusion, naturally, whether to follow, to listen to that teacher, to that guru, to that philosopher, so you begin to depend on yourself, thinking you are free to choose. The background of choice is invariably confusion. Aren't you confused when you choose? Aren't you uncertain when you pick one amongst all these? So your choice is essentially the outcome of confusion.[75]

I THINK IT MUST BE FAIRLY OBVIOUS to most of us that what we think is conditioned. Whatever your thought—however noble and wide or however limited and petty—it is conditioned, and if you further that thought there can be no freedom of thought. Thought itself is conditioned because thought is the reaction of memory, and memory is the residue of all your experiences, which in turn are the result of your conditioning. If we realize that all thinking, at whatever level, is conditioned, then we will see that thinking is not the means of breaking through this limitation—which does not mean that we must go into some blank or speculative silence.

Actually the fact is—is it not?—that every thought, every feeling, every action is conformative, conditioned, influenced. For instance, a saint comes along and by his rhetoric, gestures, looks, by quoting this and that to you, influences you. And we want to be influenced and are afraid to move away from every form of influence and see if we can go deeply and discover if there is a state of being which is not the result of influence.

Why are we influenced? In politics, as you know, it is the job of the politician to influence us; and every book, every teacher, every guru—the more powerful, the more eloquent, the better we like it—imposes his thought, his way of life, his manner of conduct upon us. So life is a battle of ideas, a battle of influences, and your mind is the field of the battle. The politician wants your mind; the guru wants your mind; the saint says, do this and not that, and he also wants your mind; and every tradition, every form of habit or custom, influences, shapes, guides, controls your mind. I think that is fairly obvious. It would be absurd to deny it.

We are saying that a mind that is influenced, shaped, authority-bound, obviously can never be free; and whatever it thinks, however lofty its ideals, however subtle and deep, it is still conditioned. I think it is very important to understand that the mind, through time, through experience, through the many thousands of yesterdays, is shaped, conditioned, and that thought is not the way out. Which does not mean that you must be thoughtless, on the contrary. When you are capable of understanding very profoundly, very deeply, extensively, widely, subtly, then only will you fully recognize how petty thinking is, how small thought is. Then there is a breaking down of the wall of that conditioning.

So can we not see the fact that all thought is conditioned? Whether it is the thought of the communist, capitalist, Hindu, Buddhist, or the person who is speaking, thinking is conditioned. And obviously the mind is the result of time, the result of the reactions of a thousand years and of yesterday, of a second ago and ten years ago; the mind is the result of the period in which you have learnt and suffered and of all the influences of the past and present. Now such a mind, obviously, cannot be free, and yet that is what we are seeking, is it not?

Being discontented when young, being dissatisfied with things as they are, with the stupidities of traditional values, we gradually, as we grow older, fall into the old patterns which society has established, and we get lost. It is very diffi-cult to keep the pure discontent, the discontent which says: this is not enough; there must be something else. We all know that feeling, the feeling of otherness, which we soon translate as God, or Nirvana, and we read a book about it and get lost. But this feeling of otherness, the search, the inquiry for it—that, I think, is the beginning of the real urge to be free from all these political, religious, and traditional influences, and to break through this wall.

Surely there are several kinds of freedom. There is political freedom; there is the freedom which knowledge gives, when you know how to do things, the know-how; the freedom of a wealthy man who can go around the world; the freedom of capacity, to be able to write, to express oneself, to think clearly. Then there is the freedom from something: freedom from oppression, freedom from envy, freedom from tradition, from ambition, and so on. And then there is the freedom which is gained, we hope, at the end—at the end of the discipline, at the end of acquiring virtue, at the end of effort, the ultimate freedom we hope to get by certain things.

So, the freedom that capacity gives, the freedom from something and the freedom we are supposed to gain at the end of a virtuous life—those are types of freedom we all know. Now are not those various freedoms merely reactions? When you say: "I want to be free from anger," that is merely a reaction; it is not freedom from anger. And the freedom which you think that you will get at the end of a virtuous life, by struggle, by discipline, that is also a reaction to what has been.

There is a sense of freedom which is not from anything, which has no cause, but which is a state of being free. You see, the freedom that we know is always brought about by will, is it not? I will be free; I will learn a technique; I will become a specialist; I will study, and that will give me free-dom. So we use will as a means of achieving freedom, do we not? I do not want to be poor and therefore I exercise my capacity, my will, everything to get rich. Or, I am vain and I exercise will not to be vain. So we think we shall get freedom through the exercise of will. But will does not bring freedom.

I will be, I must not be, I am going to struggle to become something, I am going to learn—all these are forms of exercising will. Now what is this will, and how is it formed? Obviously through desire. Our many desires, with their frustrations, compulsions, and fulfillments form, as it were, the threads of a cord, a rope. That is will, is it not? Your many contradictory desires together become a very strong and powerful rope with which you try to climb to success, to freedom.

Now will desire give freedom, or is the very desire for freedom the denial of it? Please watch yourselves, watch your own desires, your own ambition, your own will. And if one has no will and is merely being driven, that also is a part of will—the will to resist and go with the tide. Through that weight of desire, through that rope we hope to climb to God, to bliss or whatever it is.

So I am asking you whether your will is a liberating factor? Or, is freedom something entirely different which has nothing to do with reaction, which cannot be achieved through capacity, through thought, experience, discipline, or constant conformity? That is what all the books say, do they not? Conform to the pattern and you will be free in the end; do all these things, obey, and ultimately there will be freedom. To me, all that is sheer nonsense, because freedom is at the beginning not at the end, as I will show you.

To see something true is possible, is it not? You can see that the sky is blue—thousands of people have said so—but you can see that it is so for yourself. You can see for yourself—if you are at all sensitive—the movement of a leaf. From the very beginning there is the capacity to perceive that which is true, instinctively, not through any form of compulsion, adjustment, conformity.

I am trying to show you that a mind that is sensitive, inquiring, a mind that is really listening can perceive the truth of something immediately. But truth cannot be 'applied'. If you see the truth, it operates without your conscious effort, of its own accord.

Discontent is the beginning of freedom, and so long as you are trying to manipulate discontent, to accept authority in order that this discontent shall disappear, enter into safe channels, then you are already losing that pristine sense of real feeling.

Most of us are discontented—are we not?—either with our jobs, our relationships, or whatever we are doing. You want something to happen, to change, to move, to break through. You do not know what it is. There is a constant searching, inquiring, especially when one is young, open, sensitive. Later on, as you become old, you settle down in your habits, your job, because your family is safe, your wife will not run away. So this extraordinary flame disappears and you become respectable, petty, and thoughtless.

Freedom is a quality of the mind. That quality does not come about through very careful, respectable searchings and inquiries, through very careful analysis or putting ideas together. That is why it is important to see the truth that the freedom we are constantly demanding is always from something, such as freedom from sorrow. Not that there is no freedom from sorrow, but the demand to be free from it is merely a reaction and therefore does not free you from sorrow. The urge to be free of sorrow is born out of pain. I suffer, because of my husband, or my son, or something else; I do not like that state I am in and I want to get away from it. That desire for freedom is a reaction, it is not freedom. It is just another desirable state I want in opposition to *what is*.

The man who can travel around the world because he has plenty of money is not necessarily free; nor is the man who is clever or efficient, for his wanting to be free is again merely a reaction. Can I not see that freedom, liberation, cannot be learned or acquired or sought after through any reaction? Therefore I must understand the reaction, and I must also understand that freedom does not come through any effort of will.

Will and freedom are contradictory, as thought and freedom are contradictory. Thought cannot produce freedom because thought is conditioned. Economically you can, perhaps, arrange the world so that man can be more comfortable, have more food, clothing, and shelter, and you may think that is freedom. Those are necessary and essential things, but that is not the totality of freedom. Freedom is a state and quality of mind. And it is that quality we are inquiring into. Without that quality, do what you will, cultivate all the virtues in the world, you will not have that freedom.

How is that sense of otherness, that quality of mind to come about? You cannot cultivate it because the moment you use your brain you are using thought, which is limited. Whether it is the thought of the Buddha or anyone else, all thought is limited. So our inquiry must be negative; we must come to that freedom obliquely, not directly. That freedom is not to be sought after aggressively, is not to be cultivated by denials, disciplines, by checking yourself, torturing yourself, by doing various exercises and all the rest of it. It must come without your knowing, like virtue.

Cultivated virtue is not virtue; the virtue which is true virtue is not self-conscious. Surely a man who has cultivated humility, who, because of his conceit, vanity, arrogance has made himself humble, such a man has no true sense of humility. Humility is a state in which the mind is not conscious of its own quality, as a flower which has fragrance is not conscious of its own perfume. This freedom cannot be got through any form of discipline, nor can a mind which is undisciplined understand it. You use discipline to produce a result, but freedom is not a result. If it is a result, it is no longer free because it has been produced.

How is the mind, which is full of multitudinous influences, compulsions, various forms of contradictory desires, the product of time, how is that mind to have the quality of freedom? We know that all the things that I have been talking about are not freedom. They are all manufactured by the mind under various stresses, compulsions, and influences. If I can approach it negatively, in the very awareness that all this

188

is not freedom, then the mind is already disciplined—but not disciplined to achieve a result.

The mind says, I must discipline myself in order to achieve a result. But such discipline does not bring freedom. It brings a result because you have a motive, a cause which produces the result, but that result is never freedom, it is only a reaction. Now, if I begin to understand the operations of that kind of discipline, then, in the very process of understanding, inquiring, going into it, my mind is truly disciplined. The exercise of will to produce a result is called discipline; whereas, the understanding of the whole significance of will, of discipline, and of what we call result demands a mind that is extraordinarily clear and 'disciplined' not by the will but through negative understanding.

So, negatively, I have understood the whole problem of what is not freedom. I have examined it, I have searched my heart and my mind, the recesses of my being, to understand what freedom means, and I see that none of these things we have described is freedom because they are all based on desire, compulsion, will, on what I will get at the end, and they are all reactions. I see factually that they are not freedom. Therefore, because I have understood those things, my mind is open to find out or receive that which is free.

So, my mind has a quality which is not that of a disciplined mind seeking a result, nor that of the undisciplined mind which wanders about; but it has understood, negatively, both *what is* and what should be, and so can perceive, can understand that freedom which is not from something, that freedom which is not a result.

The universe cannot enter into the petty mind; the immeasurable cannot come to a mind that knows measurement. So our whole inquiry is how to break through the measurement—which does not mean I must go off to an ashram, become neurotic, devotional, and all that nonsense.

And here—if I may say so—what is important is the teaching and not the teacher. The person who speaks here at the moment is not important; throw him overboard. What is important is what is being said. So the mind only knows the measurable, the compass of itself, the frontiers, ambitions, hopes, desperation, misery, sorrows, and joys. Such a mind cannot invite freedom. All that it can do is to be aware of itself and not condemn what it sees; not condemn the ugly or cling to the beautiful, but see *what is*.

The mere perception of *what is*, is the beginning of the breaking down of the measurement of the mind, of its frontiers, its patterns—just to see things as they are. Then you will find that the mind can come to that freedom involuntarily, without knowing. This transformation in the mind itself is the true revolution. All other revolutions are reactions, even though they use the word *freedom* and promise utopia, the heavens, everything. There is only true revolution in the quality of the mind.[76]

I AM NOT AT ALL SURE that most of us want to be completely free. Rather, we should like to keep some pleasurable, satisfying, complex ideologies and gratifying formulas. We should of course like to be free of those things that are painful—the ugly memories, painful experiences, and so on.

We all say we would like to be free, but I think that before we pursue that desire with which our inclinations or tendencies confront us, we should understand the nature and the structure of freedom. Is it freedom when you are free from something, free from pain, free from some kind of anxiety; or is not freedom itself entirely different from freedom from something? One can be free from anger, perhaps from jealousy, but is not freedom from something a reaction and therefore not freedom at all?

Is not freedom something entirely different from any reaction, any inclination, any desire? One can be free from dogma very easily, by analyzing, kicking it out, yet the motive for that freedom from a dogma contains its own reaction, doesn't it? The motive, the desire to be free from a dogma, may be that it is no longer convenient, no longer fashionable, no longer reasonable, no longer popular; circumstances are against it and therefore you want to be free from it; these are merely reactions.

Is reaction away from anything freedom—or is freedom something entirely different from reaction, standing by itself without any motive, not dependent upon any inclination, tendency, and circumstance? Is there such a thing as that kind of freedom?

Can a leader, spiritual or political, promise freedom at the end of something—for can freedom which comes about through discipline, through conformity, through acceptance that promises the ideal through the following of that ideal, be freedom? Or is freedom a state of mind which is so intensely active, vigorous, that it throws away every form of dependence, slavery, conformity, and acceptance?

Does the mind want such freedom? Such freedom implies complete solitude, a state of mind which is not dependent on circumstantial stimulation, ideas, experience. Freedom of that kind obviously means aloneness, solitude.

Can the mind brought up in a culture that is so dependent upon environment, on its own tendencies, inclinations, ever find that freedom which is completely alone? It is only in such solitude that there can be relationship with another; in it there is no friction, no dominance, no dependence. Please, you have to understand this; it is not just a verbal conclusion, which you accept or deny. Is this what each individual demands and insists upon—a freedom in which there is no leadership, no tradition, no authority?

Otherwise there is not freedom; otherwise when you say you are free from something, it is merely a reaction, which, because it is a reaction, is going to be the cause of another reaction. One can have a chain of reactions, accepting each reaction as a freedom, but that chain is not freedom; it is a continuity of the modified past to which the mind clings.

Freedom is complete in itself, it is not a reaction, it is not an ideological conclusion. Freedom implies complete solitude, an inward state of mind that is not dependent on any stimulus, on any knowledge; it is not the result of any experience or conclusion. In understanding freedom we also understand what is implied in solitude. Most of us, inwardly, are never alone. There is a difference between isolation, cutting oneself off, and aloneness, solitude.

We know what it is to be isolated, to have built a wall around oneself, a wall of resistance, a wall which we have built in order never to be vulnerable. Or we may live in a dreamy idiotic ideology, which has no validity at all. All these bring about self-isolation, and in our daily life, in the office, at home, in our sexual relationships, in every activity, this process of self-isolation is going on. That form of isolation, and living in an ivory tower of ideology, has nothing whatsoever to do with solitude, with aloneness. The state of solitude, aloneness, can only come about when there is freedom from the psychological structure of society, which we have built through our reactions and of which we are.

In understanding total freedom we come upon the sense of complete solitude. I feel that it is only a mind that has understood this solitude that can have relationship in which there is no conflict whatsoever. But if we create an image of what we think is solitude and establish that as the basis of solitude in ourselves, and from that try to find a relationship, then such relationship will only bring about conflict.

We human beings—who have lived so long, gathered so much experience—are secondhand entities, there is nothing original. We are contaminated by every kind of torture, conflict, obedience, acceptance, fear, jealousy, anxiety, and therefore there is not that quality of aloneness.

We as human beings, as we are, are only a result, a psychological product. All our relationships are based on what has been, or what should be, therefore all relationship is a conflict, a battlefield. If one would understand what is right relationship, one must inquire into the nature and the structure of solitude, which is to be completely alone. But that word alone creates an image—watch yourself, you will see. When you use that word *alone*, you have already a formula, an image, and you try to live up to that image, to that formula. But the word or the image is not the fact. One has to understand and live with that which actually is.

Understanding solitude—if you really know what it means and live in that state—is really quite extraordinary, because then the mind is always fresh and is not dependent upon inclination, tendency, nor guided by circumstance. In understanding solitude you will begin to understand the necessity of living with yourself as you actually are.

In observing myself I find I am jealous, anxious, or envious—I realize that. Now I want to live with that because it is only when I live with something intimately that I begin to understand it. But to live with my envy, with my anxiety, is one of the most difficult things. I see that the moment I get used to it, I am not living with it.

There is that river and I can see it every day, hear the sound of it, the lapping of the water, but after two or three days I have got used to it and I don't always hear it. I can have a picture in the room, I have looked at it every day, at the beauty, the color, the various depths and shadows, the quality of it; yet, having looked at it for a week I have lost it, I have got used to it. And the same happens with the mountains, with the valleys, the rivers, the trees, with the family, with my wife, with my husband.

But to live with a living thing like jealousy, envy, means that I can never accept it, I can never get used to it—I must care for it as I would care for a newly planted tree. I must protect it against the sun, against the storm. In the same way, I have to live with this anxiety and envy; I must care for it, not get used to it, not condemn it. In this way I begin to love it and to care for it, which is not that I love to be envious or anxious but rather that I care for the watching. It is like living with a snake in the room; gradually I begin to see my immediate relationship to it and there is no conflict.

Can you and I live with what we actually are? Being dull, envious, fearful, thinking that we have tremendous affection when we have not, getting easily hurt, flattered, bored—can we live with these actualities, neither accepting nor denying but observing, living with them without becoming morbid, depressed, or elated? Then you will find that one of the major reasons for fear is that we don't want to live with what we are.

We have talked, first of freedom, then of solitude, and then of being aware of what we are, and also of how what we are is related to the past and has a movement towards the future, of being aware of this and of living with it, never getting used to it, never accepting it. If we understand this, not intellectually but through actually doing it, then we can ask a further question: is this freedom, this solitude, this actual coming into immediate contact with the whole structure of *what is*, to be found or to be come upon through time? That is, is freedom to be achieved through time, through a gradual process?

I am not free, because I am anxious, I am fearful, I am this, I am that, I am afraid of death, I am afraid of my neighbor, I am afraid of losing my job, I am afraid of my husband turning against me—of all the things that one has built up through life. I am not free. I can be free by getting rid of them one by one, throwing them out, but that is not freedom. Is freedom to be achieved through time? Obviously not—for the moment you introduce time there is a process, you are enslaving yourself more and more. If I am to be free from violence gradually, through the practice of nonviolence, then in the gradual practice I am sowing the seeds of violence all the time. So we are asking a very fundamental question when we ask whether freedom is to be achieved, or rather, whether it comes into being, through time?

The next question is—can one be conscious of that freedom? If one says, "I am free," then one is not free. So freedom, the freedom of which we are talking, is not something resulting from a conscious effort to achieve it. Therefore it lies beyond all, beyond the field of consciousness, and it is not a matter of time. Time is consciousness; time is sorrow; time is fear of thought.

When you say, "I have realized that complete freedom," then you certainly know, if you are really honest with yourself, that you are back where you were. It is like a man saying "I am happy," the moment he says "I am happy," he is living the memory of that which is gone. Freedom is not of time, and the mind has to look at life, which is a vast movement, without the bondage of time.[77]

194

*F*REEDOM DEMANDS SPACE. There cannot be inward freedom if there is no inward space. The word *space* is different from the fact, so may I suggest that you don't seize upon that word and get caught in trying to analyze or define it.

Now, can we put to ourselves the question: what is space?—and remain there, not trying to define the word, not trying to feel our way into it, or to inquire into it, but rather to see what it means nonverbally? Freedom and space go together. To most of us, space is the emptiness around an object—around a chair, around a building, around a person, or around the contours of the mind.

Most of us know space only because of the object. There is an object, and around it there is what we call space. There is this tent [*the talk is taking place in a large tent*], and within and around it there is space. There is space around that tree, around that mountain. We know space only within the four walls of a building, or outside the building, or around some object. Similarly, we know space inwardly only from the center which looks out at it. There is a center, the image, if I may go back to that word—and again, the word *image* is not the fact—and around this center there is space; so we know space only because of the object within that space.

Now, is there space without the object, without the center from which you as a human being are looking? Space, as we know it, has to do with design, structure; it exists in the relationship of one structure to another structure, one center to another center. Now, if space exists only because of the object, or because the mind has a center from which it is looking out, then that space is limited, and therefore in that space there is no freedom. To be free in a prison is not freedom. To be free of a certain problem within the four walls of one's relationships—that is, within the limited space of one's own image, one's own thoughts, activities, ideas, conclusions—is not freedom.

Please, may I once again suggest that through the words of the speaker you observe the limited space which you have created around yourself as a human being in relationship with another; as a human being living in a world of destruction and brutality; as a human being in relationship to a particular society. Observe your own space, see how limited it is. I do not mean the size of the room in which you live, whether it is small or big—that is not what I am talking about. I mean the inner space which each one of us has created around his own image, around a center, around a conclusion. So the only space we know is the space which has an object as its center.

Now, to understand freedom in relationship, one must go into this question of what is space; because the minds of most of us are small, petty, limited. We are heavily conditioned—conditioned by religion, by the society in which we live, by our education, by technology; we are limited, forced to conform to a certain pattern, and one sees that there is no freedom within that circumscribed area. But one demands freedom—complete freedom, not just partial freedom. Living in a prison cell for twenty-four hours a day, and going occasionally into the prison yard to walk around there—that is not freedom. As a human being living in the present society, with all its confusion, misery, conflict, torture, one demands freedom; and this demand for freedom is a healthy, normal thing.

Living in society—living in relationship with your family, with your property, with your ideas—what does it mean to be free? Can the mind ever be free if it hasn't got limitless space within itself—space not created by an idea of space, not created by an image which has a certain limited space around itself as the center? Surely, as a human being one has to find out the relationship that exists between freedom and space.

It is very important to find out for ourselves what space is, otherwise we shall always be in conflict with each other, in revolt against society. Merely to give up smoking, or to become a 'beatnik' or God knows what else, has no meaning, because those are all just forms of revolt within the prison.

Now, we are trying to find out if there is such a thing as freedom which is not a revolt—freedom which is not an ideational creation of the mind but a fact. And to find that out, one must inquire profoundly into the question of space. A petty little bourgeois, middle-class mind—or an aristocratic mind, which is also petty—may think it is free; but it is not free because it is living within the limits of its own space, the confining space created by the image in which it functions.

You cannot have order without freedom, and you cannot have freedom without space. Space, freedom, and order—the three go together, they are not separate.

Order is virtue, and virtue or goodness cannot flower in any society which is always in contradiction with itself. Outside influences—economic adjustment, social reform, technological progress, going to Mars, and all the rest of it— cannot possibly produce order. What produces order is inquiry into freedom—not intellectual inquiry, but doing the actual work of breaking down our conditioning, our limiting prejudices, our narrow ideas; breaking down the whole psy- chological structure of society, of which we are part.

Unless you break through all that, there is no freedom, and therefore there is no order. It is like a small mind trying to understand the immensity of the world, of life, of beauty. It cannot. It can imagine, it can write poems about it, paint pic- tures, but the reality is different from the word, different from the image, the symbol, the picture.

Order can come about only through the awareness of dis- order. You cannot create order—please do see this fact. You can only be aware of disorder, outwardly as well as inwardly. A disordered mind cannot create order because it doesn't know what it means. It can only react to what it thinks is disorder by creating a pattern, which it calls 'order', and then conforming to that pattern. But if the mind is conscious of the disorder in which it lives—which is being aware of the negative, not projecting the so-called positive—then order becomes something extraordinarily creative, moving, living.

Order is not a pattern which you follow day after day. To follow a pattern which you have established, to practice it day after day, is disorder—the disorder of effort, of conflict, of greed, of envy, of ambition, the disorder of all the petty little human beings who have created and been conditioned by the present society.

Now, can one become aware of disorder—aware of it without choosing, without saying, "This is disorder, and that is order"? Can one be choicelessly aware of disorder? This demands extraordinary intelligence, sensitivity; and in that choiceless awareness there is also a discipline which is not mere conformity.

When one examines the whole structure and meaning of discipline, whether it is imposed discipline or self-discipline, one sees that it is a form of outward or inward conformity or adjustment to a pattern, to a memory, to an experience. And we revolt against that discipline. Every human mind revolts against the stupid kind of conformity, whether established by dictators, priests, saints, gods, or whatever they are. And yet one sees that there must be some kind of discipline in life—a discipline which is not mere conformity, which is not adjustment to a pattern, which is not based on fear, and all the rest of it; because if there is no discipline at all, one can't live.

One has to find out if there is a discipline which is not conformity; because conformity destroys freedom, it never brings freedom into being. Look at the organized religions throughout the world, the political parties. It is obvious that conformity destroys freedom, and we don't have to labor the point. Either you see it, or you don't see it; it is up to you.

The discipline of conformity, which is created by the fear of society and is part of the psychological structure of society, is immoral and disorderly, and we are caught in it. Now, can the mind find out if there is a certain movement of discipline which is not a process of controlling, shaping, conforming? To find that out, one has to be aware of this extraordinary disorder, confusion, and misery in which one lives; and to be aware of it—not fragmentarily but totally and therefore choicelessly—that in itself is discipline.

If I am fully aware of what I am doing, if I am choicelessly aware of the movement of my hand, for example, that very awareness is a form of discipline in which there is no conformity. You cannot understand this just verbally, you have actually to do it within yourself.

Order can come about only through this sense of awareness in which there is no choice, and which is therefore a total awareness, a complete sensitivity to every movement of thought. This total awareness itself is discipline without conformity; therefore, out of this total awareness of disorder, there is order. The mind hasn't produced order.

To have order, which is the flowering of goodness and of beauty, there must be freedom; and there is no freedom if you have no space.

So the mind has to discover by hard work, and not just by listening to some words, that there is in fact space without a center. When once that has been found, there is freedom, there is order, and then goodness and beauty flower in the human mind.

Discipline, order, freedom, and space cannot exist without the understanding of time. It is very interesting to inquire into the nature of time—time by the watch, time as yesterday, today, and tomorrow, the time in which you work, and the time in which you sleep. But there is also time which is not by the watch, and that is much more difficult to understand.

We look to time as a means of bringing about order. We say, "Give us a few more years and we will be good, we will create a new generation, a marvelous world." Or we talk about creating a different type of human being, one who will be totally communist, totally this or totally that. So we look to time as a means of bringing about order, but if one observes, one sees that time only breeds disorder.[78]

THERE MUST BE A GAP between the old and something new that may come into being. There must be a gap. And that gap takes place when you see the whole significance of the old—that the old cannot possibly give birth to the new. We all want the new because we are fed up with the old, bored; we know what the old is and, wanting the new, we don't know how to break the chain. There are gurus, teachers, and all the absurd people who say, "I'll teach you how to break the chain." And their breaking the chain is still within the pattern of thought. They say, "Do this, don't do that, follow this, think that," but they are still caught within the system of thought.

To have an insight into that doesn't require time. You see instantly how absurd this whole religious structure is, all the organization around it, the pope, the bishops—you follow—the absurdity of all that. Grown up people playing with childish things. If you have an insight into that, it is finished. Then you ask: how am I to have an insight? Which means you haven't actually listened. You are still holding on to your old skirts of the churches, beliefs, and ideologies, and you say: "I can't let go because I am afraid." "What will my neighbor think?" "I will lose my job." So you don't want to listen, so that is the problem. Not how to acquire perception, not how to come by insight, but rather that you don't listen to the danger of the whole thing which thought has built. And to have the insight you have to listen, you have to let go and listen.[79]

Now to be free of attachment doesn't mean its opposite—detachment. When we are attached we know the pain of attachment, the anxiety of it, and we say, "For god's sake, I must detach myself from all this horror." So the battle of detachment begins, the conflict. Whereas if you observe, are aware of the fact and the word, the word *attachment* and freedom from that word, which is the feeling, then observe that feeling without any judgment. Observe it. Then you will see out of that total observation there is quite a different movement taking place, which is neither attachment or detachment.

Can you be free of this attachment so that there is a responsibility which is not a duty? Then what is love when there is no attachment? Look, if you are attached to a nationality, you worship the isolation of nationality, which is a form of glorified tribalism. You are attached to it. What does that do? It breaks it up, doesn't it? I am attached to my nationality as a Hindu, tremendously, and you are attached to

200

Germany, France, Italy, England. We are separate; and the wars, and all the complexity of all that goes on. Now if there is no attachment, and you have no attachment, what takes place? Is that love?

So attachment separates. I am attached to my belief, and you are attached to your belief, therefore there is separation. Just see the consequences of it, the implications of it. So where there is attachment, there is separation, and therefore there is conflict. Where there is conflict, there cannot possibly be love.

And what is the relationship of a man and a woman? What is his relationship to another when there is freedom from attachment, all the implications of it. Is that the beginning—I am just using the word *beginning*, don't jump on it—is that the beginning of compassion? You understand? When there is no nationality, and there is no attachment to any belief whatsoever, to any conclusion, to any ideal, then a human being is a free human being. And his relationship with another is out of freedom—isn't it?—out of love, out of compassion.

It is absolutely necessary to be free to observe, free from one's prejudices, from one's longing, from one's fears—all that which we have talked about endlessly. Can the mind be completely without movement? Because if there is movement there is distortion. So can the mind be completely still? And one finds it terribly difficult because thought comes in immediately, so one says, "I must control thought." The controller is the controlled—we have been through all that, I won't go into it. When you see that, that the thinker is the thought, the controller is the controlled, the observer is the observed, then there is no movement. One realizes that anger is part of the observer who says, "I am angry," so anger and the observer are the same. That is clear, that is simple. In the same way, the thinker who wants to control thought is still thought. When one realizes that, the movement of thought stops.

When there is no movement of any kind in the mind, then naturally the mind is still, without effort, without compulsion, without will, without all that. It is naturally still, not cultivated stillness, because that is mechanical, which is not stillness, which is just an illusion of stillness. So there is free-dom—freedom implies all that we have talked about—and in that freedom there is silence, which means no movement. Then you can observe—then there is observation; then there is only observation, not the observer observing. So there is only observation out of total silence, complete stillness of mind. Then what takes place? Then there is the operation of intelligence, isn't there?

Look, I'll show you. We said attachment implies great pain, anxiety, fear, and therefore deepening of possession. To see that is part of intelligence, isn't it? To see the nature of attachment and all its implications, to have an insight into it, is intelligence. I am not talking of the cunning intelligence of thought that says, "How true that is." If you see all the implications of attachment and see the danger of attachment, that perception is intelligence. That's all. That's all.[80]

N O T E S

INTRODUCTION

1. M. Lutyens, *The Years of Awakening*, p. 170.
2. Ibid., pp. 171–72.
3. *The Dissolution of the Order of the Star*, 3 August 1929.

DIALOGUE

4. Bombay, 3d public talk, 29 January 1983.
5. *Talk and Dialogues Saanen 1967*, 1st public talk, 9 July 1967.
6. Madras, 5th public talk, 19 January 1952.

AUTHORITY

7. *Talks and Dialogues Saanen 1967*, 10th public talk, 30 July 1967.
8. Bombay, 4th public talk, 20 February 1957.
9. *The Wholeness of Life*, part 2, chapter 2 (originally 2d public talk, Saanen, 12 July 1977).
10. *Education and the Significance of Life*, chapter 3, "Intellect, Authority, and Intelligence."
11. Bombay, 4th public talk, 5 March 1950.

AS A HUMAN BEING

12. *The Awakening of Intelligence*, part 4, chapter 1 (1st conversation with Swami Venkatesananda, Saanen, 25 July 1969).
13. Brockwood Park, 2d conversation with Prof. Bohm, Mr. Narayan, and two Buddhist scholars, 23 June 1978.
14. New Delhi, 10th public talk, 11 March 1959.

FEAR

15. Saanen, 6th public talk, 2 August 1962.
16. Saanen, 4th public dialogue, 7 August 1971.
17. Bombay, 3rd public talk, 29 January 1983.
18. *Beyond Violence*, part 2, chapter 1 (also San Diego State College, 2d public talk, 6 April 1970).
19. Brockwood Park, 2d conversation with Mary Zimbalist, 5 October 1984.
20. Varanasi, 5th public talk, 10 January 1962.
21. New Delhi, 4th public talk, 24 February 1960.

LONELINESS
22. Madras, 5th public talk, 30 December 1964.
23. Ojai, 3d public talk, 8 April 1978.
24. Amsterdam, 4th public talk, 23 May 1955.
25. Brussels, 4th public talk, 23 June 1956.
26. Bombay, 5th public talk, 22 February 1953.

DISCONTENT
27. *This Matter of Culture*, chapter 25 (also called *Think on These Things*).
28. Ibid.
29. Bombay, 5th public talk, 22 February 1953.
30. *Tradition and Revolution*, dialogue 1, New Delhi, 12 December 1970.

PRIDE/AMBITION
31. *Life Ahead*, part 1, chapter 10.
32. Banaras, India, 8th talk to students at Rajghat School, 13 January 1954.
33. *Life Ahead*, part 1, chapter 7.
34. New Delhi, 3d public talk, 13 January 1961.
35. Bombay, 9th public talk, 8 March 1953.
36. London, 1st public talk, 5 June 1962.

ANGER
37. *Commentaries on Living Series I*, chapter 30, "Anger."
38. Bombay, 2d public question and answer meeting, 7 February 1985.
39. *Freedom From The Known*, chapter 6.
40. Saanen, 3d public dialogue, 6 August 1971.
41. Saanen, 2d public discussion, 3 August 1972.
42. Saanen, 3d public talk, 11 July 1963.

GUILT
43. Ojai, 1st question and answer meeting, 14 May 1985.
44. Bombay, 2d public talk, 10 February 1957.
45. Saanen, 1st public dialogue, 1 August 1973.

DESIRE
46. Bombay, 2d public talk, 10 February 1957.
47. Saanen, 4th public talk, 17 July 1977.
48. *The First and Last Freedom*, question 21.
49. Brockwood Park, 2d public question and answer meeting, 30 August 1979.

HAPPINESS

50. Ojai, 14th public talk, 28 August 1949.
51. *Commentaries on Living Series I*, chapter 85, "Sensation and Happiness."
52. Bombay, 6th public talk, 25 February 1953.
53. Rajghat, 10th talk to boys and girls, 21 December 1952.
54. *Talks and Dialogues Sydney 1970*, 3d public talk, 25 November 1970.
55. Ommen, 5th public talk, 6 August 1937.
56. *Krishnamurti's Journal* (Ojai, 8 April 1975).
57. *Flight of the Eagle*, chapter 8, Paris, 5th public talk, 24 April 1969.

SELF AND IDENTIFICATION

58. Stockholm, 4th public talk, 22 May 1956.
59. Madras, 5th public talk, 19 January 1952.
60. Ojai, 1st public talk, 7 April 1946.
61. Hamburg, 2d public talk, 6 September 1956.
62. *Exploration into Insight*, "Energy and the Cultivation of the Field."
63. Madras, 12th public talk, 10 February 1952.
64. *Talks and Dialogues Sydney 1970*, 2d public dialogue, 19 November 1970.
65. Brockwood Park, 3d conversation with Bohm, Narayan, and two Buddhist scholars, 23 June 1978.
66. *Beginnings of Learning*, part 1, chapter 10 (school dialogue, Brockwood Park, 19 June 1971).
67. Madras, 12th public talk, 10 February 1952.
68. Ojai, 5th public talk, 5 May 1946.
69. Ojai, 4th public talk, 28 April 1946.
70. Ojai, 6th public talk, 12 May 1946.
71. Bombay, 11th public talk, 21 March 1948.
72. Madras, 11th public talk, 28 December 1947.
73. Brockwood Park, 2d public question and answer meeting, 30 August 1979.
74. Ojai, 4th public talk, 28 April 1946.

FREEDOM

75. San Francisco, 1st public talk, 20 March 1975.
76. Poona, 5th public talk, 21 September 1958.
77. *Talk and Dialogues Saanen 1967*, 5th public talk, 18 July 1967.
78. Saanen, 4th public talk, 18 July 1965.
79. Brockwood Park, 1st public talk, 9 September 1972.
80. Saanen, 5th public dialogue, 1 August 1976.

LIST OF
PUBLICATIONS

Fire in the Mind: Dialogues with J. Krishnamurti
Flame of Attention
A Flame of Learning
Flight of the Eagle
Freedom from the Known
Freedom, Love and Action
From Darkness to Light
Future Is Now
Future of Humanity
Krishnamurti for Beginners
Krishnamurti at Rahjghat
Krishnamurti in India 1970–71
Krishnamurti on Action
Krishnamurti: On Conflict
Krishnamurti on Education
Krishnamurti: On Fear
Krishnamurti: On Freedom
Krishnamurti: On God
Krishnamurti on Individual and Society
Krishnamurti: On Learning and Knowledge
Krishnamurti: On Living and Dying
Krishnamurti: On Love and Loneliness
Krishnamurti: On Mind and Thought
Krishnamurti on Mirror of Relationship
Krishnamurti: On Nature and Environment
Krishnamurti: On Relationship
Krishnamurti: On Right Livelihood
Krishnamurti on Social Responsibility
Krishnamurti: On Truth
Krishnamurti on the Meditative Mind
Krishnamurti to Himself: His Last Journal
Krishnamurti's Journal
Krishnamurti's Notebook
Krishnamurti in India 1974–75
Last Talks at Saanen 1985
Letters to the Schools, Vol. 1
Letters to the Schools, Vol. 2
Life Ahead
Meditations 1979
Meeting Life
Mind Without Measure
Network of Thought
Questions and Answers
Questioning Krishnamurti
Second Penguin Reader

Talks and Dialogues, Saanen 1967
Talks and Dialogues, Saanen 1968
Talks and Dialogues, Sydney 1970
Talks in Europe 1967
Talks in Europe 1968
Talks in Saanen 1974
Talks with American Students
The Impossible Question
The Only Revolution
The Urgency of Change
The Book of Life
The World of Peace
Things of the Mind
Think on These Things
Tradition and Revolution
Truth and Actuality
Washington DC Talks 1985
Way of Intelligence
Wholeness of Life
You Are the World

SECONDARY SOURCES: BIOGRAPHIES AND MEMOIRS

Friedrich Grohe. *The Beauty of the Mountain: Memories of Krishnamurti*
Pupul Jayakar. *Krishnamurti: A Biography*
Mary Lutyens. *Krishnamurti: The Years of Awakening*
Mary Lutyens. *Krishnamurti: The Years of Fulfillment*
Mary Lutyens. *Krishnamurti: The Open Door*
Mary Lutyens. *Krishnamurti: His Life and Death*
Stuart Holroyd. *Krishnamurti: The Man, the Mystery, the Message*
Sydney Fields. *Krishnamurti: The Reluctant Messiah*
Evelyne Blau. *Krishnamurti: 100 Years*
Asit Chandmal. *One Thousand Moons*
Asit Chandmal. *One Thousand Suns*
Michael Krohnen. *The Kitchen Chronicles: 1001 Lunches with J. Krishnamurti*

INDEX

meeting of, 68
and passion, relation
between, 69, 70
types of, 68–69
Theosophical Society,
Theosophy, xv–xvi, xvii,
xviii
thought
as conditioned, 184, 188
ending of, 25, 28
and memory, 176, 183
place of, 29–30
and pleasure, role of, 151
and self, 22–23, 25, 28,
150
and senses, identification
with, 147–49
and thinker, relation
between, 167–68,
173–74
truth, 108, 144, 180, 187

Turgenev, Ivan, xvi

the unconscious, 84, 87–88
unconditioning of, 84
understanding, 163–66

values, creation of, 20
violence
and anger, 94–95
and desire, 91
freeing from, 92–95
and separation, 94
understanding of, 92–94
and will, 90–91, 121
virtue, pursuing of, 131–32,
141, 188

Wilkins, Maurice, xix
Wodehouse, P. G., xvi
world, bringing change to, 6,
33, 62